To Joyce and Warren,
The Best House Guests Ever!..
With Best Blessings
Love,
Julia (aka Miss Paddy)

Mrs. Paddy's Political Parodies

A Tea Party Songbook for the New Revolution

Mrs. Paddy

authorHOUSE®

AuthorHouse™
1663 Liberty Drive
Bloomington, IN 47403
www.authorhouse.com
Phone: 1-800-839-8640

© 2009 Mrs. Paddy. All rights reserved.

No part of this book may be reproduced, stored in a retrieval system, or transmitted by any means without the written permission of the author.

First published by AuthorHouse 5/11/2009

ISBN: 978-1-4389-8005-8 (e)
ISBN: 978-1-4389-8003-4 (sc)
ISBN: 978-1-4389-8004-1 (hc)

Printed in the United States of America
Bloomington, Indiana

This book is printed on acid-free paper.

This book is dedicated to all my Townhall friends:
the Squad, the Chatroom,
and especially, GunnyG,
who first encouraged me to publish this book.
Thank you all for your support!

I also thank my husband for his unwavering support!
Without you there is no song in my heart.

Table of Contents

Foreword xv

Chapter One: Tea Party Songs

Revolution	2
There's a Yellow Flag a Waving	4
Battle Hymn of the Tea Parties	6
We're Happy We're Conservatives!	7
Conservative Things	9
My Day to Yell	11
Mrs. Paddy's 50 Ways to Save our Country	12
Keep on Knockin' Him Daily	14
Flintlocks!	16
Thank the Lord that we Still Have our Guns	17
Thanks for the Cap and Trade	19

Chapter Two: Political Hot Buttons

Lib'ruls	22
LIBS!	23
Liberals in the Dark	24
Tellin' Ya Lies!	26
The Night the Lights Went Out in Congress	28
When Congress is in Session	30
The 110th Congress	31
Those Pols are Deranged	33
Most Writers Spin His Lies	35
Oh I'm Snarling	36
Drunken Sailors!	38
Porkbusters	40
Ee I Ee I Ouch!	42
Sixteen Tons of Pork!	43
Give Back!	45
Take the Money You Bums	46
Look Out for Mr. Tax	47
Angst for the Centuries	48
Wreck of the G.O.P.	50

Oh Yes! We're the Great Pretenders	52
Flip Flop!	53
It's A Zoo	55
Getting to Know Them	57
Pop! Pols are Weasels	59
Wake Up, Smell the Coffee!	60
Dubya Said He'd Change the Tone	62
I'm the Decider	64
Rock the Vote	65
Vote the G O P	66
Stop! It's Election Day!	67
Gov Train	69
Send Them Back, Jack	71
No More Silence	72
PRESSURE	74
Come On, It's Just the Weather!	76
It's So Easy Bein' Green	77
Al Gore	78
Uncle Albert	79
It's Doo-Doo	81
Swallow the Next Episode	83
Polar Bears are Yummy	84
Greenies Tap Corn	85
Why Not Drill?	87
Drillin' Drillin' Drillin'	91
Get you Some Victimhood	93
Ebony and Ivory	95
Bad Race Relations	96
Obama Played the Race Card	98
The Reverend Jeremiah Wright	99
For Twenty Years He Listened	101
Get Back Honky	103
Let's Talk Some More 'bout Race	105

Chapter Three: Politicians

Jimmy Carter

That Ding A Ling	108

Jimmy Rat! 110
Welcome Back Cah-tah! 111

John Edwards
Don't Have a Neutron's Chance 112
Remix of Don't have a Neutron's Chance 114
Caught You Mr. Ed 116

Mike Huckabee
Huckabee Do Dah! 117

Elliot Spitzer
New York New York 119

Ron Blagojevich
Who Are the People with Blagojevich? 120

Hillary Rodham Clinton
Fearful, Queasy Feeling 121
She'll Spin it Easy 123
Do It My Way 125
I'm Just a Socialist 127
I Need Money 128
I Agonize 129
Be Our Guarantor 130
I've Been Through the Wringer 132
You've Got to Change 133
She's A Loser 134
She Says She is for Changin' 135
I'll Cry if I Want To 136
Boo Hoo Hoo 137
It's Too Late 138

John McCain
I'm John McCain, and I'm a RINO 139
He's McVain 140
Mistakes 142
Dems are in Disguise 143
No More Joy 144
Upside Down World 145
Only the Good Die Young 146
McCain Ain't Right 148

I Get No Kick From McCain	150
Mack the Knife	151
Big John	153
I Am the Maverick!	155
He Has a Dopey Left Agenda	157

Joe Biden

It's Biden This Time	158
The Storybook Man	160
Ballad of Obama/Biden	162

Tim Geithner

Call Me Indispensable	164

Sarah Palin

Sarah Sarah, Fills 'em with Terror	165
It's Maverick!	167
Joy We're Expressing	169
Sarah-cuda!	170
The Ballad of Palin's In	172
WeWantObama2Lose	173

Nancy Pelosi

Kind of a Hag	174
Pop Goes Pelosi	176

Chapter Four: Barack Obama

Born Me!	178
Call Me Obama	179
U Can't Touch This	181
Hey Dude!	183
You Gotta Have Hope	184
Let Barack Take You Away!	186
Why Obama?	187
Back Home to Chicago	189
Globama	191
No Thicket to Hide	193
Pay It Back	195
Say I Have Audacity	196
Ain't Never Had a Friend Like Me	197

When You Catch Obama's Star	199
Obama (Tin Man)	200
Razzle Dazzle	201
Mudcat, Mudcat	203
Obama (Cecilia)	205
Obama (La Bamba)	206
Baa Baa Black Sheep	207
Pirouettes on the Stage	208
Oh Obama!	210
I'm a Clown	211
Talk to Our Enemies	213
I'm an Appeaser	214
I Saw A Candidate!	215
Obama, Naturally	216
That Oh! Obama Spell	217
We Don't Like B.O.	218
Obama, No!	219
Who's a Bully?	221
Knick-Knack Paddy Whack!	222
The Men Who Vote: Barry Obama	224
B.O.	225
Barry Obama (Mr. Bojangles)	227
Run Run Run	229
Mr. Sandman	230
Talking 'bout Obama's Blunderland	231
Change for Fools	232
Who is that New Demagogue Obama?	233
Obama (Elvira)	234
His Name's Barack Obama	235
Flipper	237
On the Road with Obama	238
Ballad of Barack Obama	239
Go Home! B. Obama!	240
Lip Flapping Away!	242
Hello Barry!	244
He Says He is for Changin'	246
I'm Ringin' in the Change	248

Now it's a Recession!	249
I'll Follow the One	250
Blunder on Blunder	252
My Kind of Clown!	254
How Do You Solve a Problem Like Obama?	255
You Love Me 'cause I ROCK!	257
They Call His Name Obama	259
Mr. Cellophane!	261

Chapter Five: 2008 Election and New Administration

Raise Your Hand for the Man with the Plan	264
He'll Spin it Easy	266
I've been a Maverick!	268
Blunderful Hopenchangin'	270
If I Were Obama	271
Big Marshmallow!	273
Mr. Democrat	275
Barack's Magic History Tour	277
You Know They'd Rather Deal With Me!	279
ACORN	281
ACORN Keeps Fallin' on My Head	282
I'm at GITMO Terror Bastion!	283
He's Still Just B.O. To Me	285
Peggy the Moocher	287
Can't Help Feelin' It's Rigged this Time	289
His Sleaze, Hacks and Thieves	290
We Need a Little Litmus!	291
Oklobama!	293
Teleprompter Song	295
Hail to the Chief	296
Ballad of B.O.	297
Faces	298
There Are No Strings on Me!	299
If I Only Had A Brain	301
Obamalot	303
It Only Takes A Moment!	305
The Days of Whine and Moses	306

Swingin' on a Star!	307
I'm An Enemy of the State, I Am	309

Chapter Six: Patriots, Townhallers, & Fun Stuff

They're Snide!	312
I Get Around	314
Tell the Libs Off, You're the GunnyG	316
Do You Know What's In Store	318
How Do You Help a Liberal?	320
Columnists are Famous	322
Scroll on By	324
Rob Rob Rob	325
Nobody Likes a Liberal Like Sophia	327
Tony Snow	329
Love a Pun	330
He's Just Absurd!	332
America Vs Al Qaeda	334
Midnight in Montana	336
Someday When We See Rainbows	338
He Is Your Friend	340
We Built This Country	342
Sweet USA	344
Our Great Liberty	346

Foreword

This book is a compilation of parodies that I wrote for my blog at Townhall. Stop by sometime at mrspaddy.blogtownhall.com. If you post at Townhall, you may see your 'name' here. Many of you have inspired these words.

Whenever possible I have acknowledged original artists, lyricists or the musicians whose works are the springboard for these parodies. Any errors in this regard are unintentional and I apologize in advance if I have been in any way inaccurate in my attributions. I love all the music that contributed to the creation of these parodies, and thank those great artists for their inspiration. I hope these parodies will provide you as much enjoyment as I have had in writing them.

~Mrs. Paddy

Chapter One:
Tea Party Songs

Revolution
From the Beatles' "Revolution" in response to the article by Amanda Carpenter on the Senate Payout for Builders. This was originally posted on April 9, 2008, and has been updated since the election.

I say we need a revolution
Well, you know
It is time to change the pols
They say they back the Constitution
Well, you know
I'm not sure that graft's the goal.

But when you talk about why I doubt
Here they come with another big bail-out
Don't you know it's gonna be a sight
a sight, a sight

They say they've got a real solution
Well, you know
They're just bound to raise the tax
They ask us for a contribution
Well, you know
We are trumped by all the PACs

But when you want money for people who failed to plan
All I can tell you is Brother, don't give a damn.
Don't you know it's gonna be a blight
A blight, a blight
Ah
ah, ah ah, ah ah....

I say follow the Constitution
Well, you know
They all want to take our wealth
They should be in an institution
Well, you know
Now they want to subsidize your health

But if they continue to spend all our hard-earned dough
There won't be an engine in USA anymore
Don't you know I wish we could just indict
Indict, Indict, Indict
(echo and repeat)

There's a Yellow Flag a Waving
The stem for this is: The Yellow Rose of Texas

There's a Yellow Flag a Waving
It says "Don't Tread on Me"
It's here for Revolution
In this "Land of the Free"

You may talk about the Stars and Stripes
And say it's Time for TEA
But the Yellow Flag that's waving
Is as clear as A B C.

It's the sweetest flag for protests
That Patriots ever knew
It has a snake upon it
To strike a warning true

You may talk about a stimulus
Or Bail-outs for the banks-
But with Yellow Flags a waving!
We say, "Barry O. No Thanks!"

When we listened to the pundits
Say we'd make "history!"
And, "We should choose Obama
To speak for you and me."

Now we wonder why a teleprompter
Tells him what to say?
When this Yellow Flag we're waving
Is his message for today.

It's the sweetest flag for protests
That Patriots ever knew
Obama are you listening?
We Do Not Work for YOU

You may think Tea Parties aren't a threat
But don't ignore the fuss.
'Cause we are 'We the People'
And you all work for Us!

Battle Hymn of the Tea Parties
"Battle Hymn of the Republic"

Mine eyes have seen the glory of this Land of Liberty
Like in Boston when the harbor was awash in England's Tea
Now Tea Parties are in every town
From Hilo to D.C.
Our Freedom is Not Free!

Glory Glory Flags are Waving
Glory Glory Terror Braving
Glory Glory Freedom Saving
Our Freedom is Not Free!

We surely understand the Constitution is our guide
It's the bedrock of a nation that has filled our hearts with pride
We'll defend her from all enemies
No matter what the Tide
Our Freedom is Not Free!

Glory Glory Flags are Waving
Glory Glory Terror Braving
Glory Glory Freedom Saving
Our Freedom is Not Free!

In the beauty of this nation freedom reigns from sea to sea
On a hill a shining city! We defended Liberty!
Oh be swift all those who love this land!
Be vigilant and speak!
For Freedom we March On!

Fly Old Glory for our Nation!
Why? For Glory's Preservation!
Glory, Glory's Celebration!
Our Freedom is Not Free!

We're Happy We're Conservatives!
*From, Dumbo,: 'The Song of the Roustabouts'
by Oliver Wallace and Ned Washington*

Hike! Ugh! Hike! Ugh! Hike! Ugh! Hike!
We work all day, we work all night
We are the members of the Right
We're happy we're Conservatives!

Hike! Ugh! Hike! Ugh! Hike! Ugh! Hike!
So other folks can pay our share
Expand the use of Medicare
We're happy we're the Democrats!

Hike! Ugh! Hike! Ugh! Hike! Ugh! Hike!
We don't know how to spend our pay
We let the Congress tax our cares away
(We don't know how to spend our pay,
we let the Congress tax away)
We hear our politicians say
We've happy hearts, "Election Day's today!"
(We hear our politicians say "Election Day is here today")

Taxes growin' Overflowin'
Tax and Spend ain't what we need (no sir!)
Borders strengthened - ICE Defendin'
Our security!
There ain't no let up - Must get set up
Can't we right this ship of state?
Leftwards listing - Backwards drifting
Is it all too late?
Hep! Heave! Hep! Heave! Hep! Heave!
Hep! Heave! Hep! Heave! Hep! Heave!
Hep! Heave! Hep!

Sling that sludge! You're all wrong!
Work your campaigns all night long
All you black-hearted candidates!
Pullin', poundin', lyin', groundin'
Your opponents into dust
Keep on stumping!
Voters humping!
Get that vote, you think you must!
Stumpin'! Humpin'! Stumpin'! Humpin'!
Oh......

Conservative Things
From 'My Favorite Things' -Sound of Music
-Rodgers and Hammerstein

Right Wing Conspirators
Listening to Limbaugh
Second Amendment Rights
Liberals to out-draw
Eagles that fly with our flag on their wings
These are a list of Conservative things

Patriot soldiers
And Pledge of Allegiance
Reagan remembered
For being a genius
Honoring memories of Reverend King
These are a few more Conservative things

When the Libs bark
We're too right-wing
And that Bush was bad
We simply remember conservative things
And notice that we've been had!

Hannity's notions
And Colmes in a tizzy
Then Laura Ingraham
Keeps our minds busy
Reading on Townhall and blogs entering
These are a few more Conservative things

Support for our borders
Freedom of expression
Honor the flag
Proud to be an American
Standing erect as our anthem we sing
These are a few more conservative things

Not Obama
No more Clintons
Reject John McCain
We simply remember conservative things
And wonder what's here to gain?

Trusting the Founders
They knew what we needed
Keeping our taxes low
Our voices heeded
Wond'ring how Congress could get it so wrong
Weren't there conservatives there all along?

Now we're purple
No more red/blue
And I'm feeling sad
Why can't we remember conservative things
And save the great land we had!

My Day to Yell
AC/DC Highway to Hell by A. Young / M. Young / B. Scott

Listen to me
Can't you see?
We're all Ticked we're on a one-way ride!
Askin' somethin'
Leave Me Be!
Takin' everything' but not my pride!
Don't need bail-outs
Don't need Tax
Ain't nothin' that I need from you!
Cap and Trade?
Tea Party Time!
All my friends are gonna be there too!
Oh yes, it's my day to yell!
My Day to Yell!
Oh yes, It's my day to Yell!
MY DAY TO YELL!

No incumbents!
Term limits!
Some how we gotta slow them down
It's unreal
How they spin it!
Obama is a scary clown!
Hey Statesmen
Pay your dues!
Uphold the Constitution Man!
Hey Obama
Have some Tea!
We're here! This is the promised land!
And listen up! (it's) My Day to Yell
My Day to YELL
You'd better listen cause it's my day to yell
My Day to Yell
(echo and repeat)

Mrs. Paddy's 50 Ways to Save our Country
based on: Paul Simon's 50 Ways to Leave your Lover

The problem is all inside D.C. it's plain to see
The answer is easy if you value Liberty
You must stand strong in this our struggle to be Free
There must be Fifty ways to Save our Country
You see it's really not our habit to intrude
We all have lives you see, and voted for the dudes
But now we need to speak before our goose is stewed
There must be 50 ways to Save our Country
Fifty States to Save our Country!

Just send em a Fax, Max
Get on the Phone, Joan
You just need to Annoy, Roy
Just listen to me
We're under the bus, Gus
Don't they know they disgust us?
Just send em more Tea, Lee
And tell them you're FREE

They say that hope and change will be no compromise
Yet we see despotism right before our eyes
It's plain to see the Constitution they despise
There must be Fifty States to Save our Country

I say there is no time to sleep on this tonight
We must act quickly to eliminate this blight
To preserve Liberty we must embrace the Fight
There must be Fifty States to Save our Country
Fifty States! to Save our Country

Oooh, MARCH ON THE MALL, Saul
Just plan to IMPEACH, Teach
Then move to INDICT, Mike
They'll listen, you see?

We've got our GUNS, Son
And we are itching to 'GET SOME!'
Just tell em we're MAD, Dad
We need to be FREE!

Keep on Knockin' Him Daily
(Steve Miller) wrote the original "Keep On Rockin' Me Baby"

Well I've been watchin' B.O.
And I got to tell you Bro
That those lies! He tells another every day
But I got to do my part 'cause I know in my heart
I got to stand up for the U.S.A.

Well, I think he's ambitious
One might say he's pernicious
And Obama's not a friend of mine
And I know that it's fair 'cause the things that he dares
Will undermine the Constitution, yeah.

So I'll keep knockin' him daily
I'll Keep a Knockin' him Daily
I'll Keep a Knockin' him Daily
I'll Keep a Knockin' him Daily

Tea Parties in Sacramento
All the way to Orlando
Pittsburgh, Denver, and Wyoming I say
Warning B. Obama and the Animal Farm
So he can see we're in no mood to play!

Keep on a Knockin' him daily
Keep on a Knockin' him daily
Keep on a Knockin' him daily
Keep on a Knockin' him daily
Daily, Daily, Daily
Keep on Knockin'
Knockin' him daily
Keep on Knockin
Knockin' him daily
Oooooh, Yeah!

His acumen is fictitious
Every day he's capricious
Can't you see he is no friend of thine?
With Teleprompters in tow
And he can't answer to Joe
And our Constitution's on the line!

Tea Parties in Sacramento
All the way to Orlando
Pittsburgh, Denver, and Wyoming I say
Warning B. Obama and the Animal Farm
So you can see we're in no mood to play!

Keep on a Knockin' him Daily
Keep on a Knockin' him Daily
Keep on a Knockin' him Daily
Keep on a Knockin him, knockin' him, knockin'
Daily Daily Daily
Keep on a Knockin' him Daily
Keep on a Knockin' him Daily
Keep on a Knockin' him Daily

Flintlocks!
From the Flintstones Theme.

Flintlocks, Bring your Flintlocks
They're important to our sovereignty!
From our Nation's Bedrock
It's a page from our great history!

Let's look at our Constitution, please!
Before B.O. takes our Liberties!
When you've got your flintlock
We can counter the Obama!
That nightmare drama!
Just keep your powder dry!

Thank the Lord that we Still Have our Guns
*From the Musical: Annie Get Your Gun, "You Can't
Get a Man with a Gun" by Irving Berlin*

(*Prelude*)
Oh, our Founders were frightened by politicians, they say
That's why This is the country we bless
They were sure that we needed
Armed and able citizens
To keep a good bead on Congress!

They're quick on the trigger
With projects ever bigger
And we all soon will be undone
And their score with the raters
Is like Down on elevators
Thank the Lord that we still have our guns!

When they go to Congress
They suddenly forget us
Yes, they need all the hype they've spun
Cause they don't pass our muster
When they rule it's a 'cluster'
Thank the Lord that we still have our guns!

We need guns! We need Guns!
Thank the Lord that we still have our guns!

If we go to battle
Soon after they all prattle
That they ne'er gave a vote, they Run!
But if we are commissioned
We carry out our mission
Oh we must hold the line,
Though they whine all the time!
Thank the Lord that we still have our guns!

They're fools, knaves and spineless
In fact they all are mindless
Soon as they get to Washington
'Cause they just want th'election
To uphold their selection
Thank the Lord that we still have our guns.
Those folks with the purse-strings
Must think that they are our Kings
'Cause they spend til the day is done.
But you'd think they'd not trifle
With those who carry rifles
Thank the Lord that we still have our guns!

We need guns! We need guns!
Thank the Lord that we still have our guns!

Our nation is Mighty
Although our pols are flighty
Check and Balance has kept us one
But we will not surrender
With our rifles we'll defend her
For our land of the Free
We'll defend you and me
Thank the Lord that we still have our guns!

Thanks for the Cap and Trade
*Thanks Bob Hope for your theme song. Original
song by Leo Robin and Ralph Rainger.*

Thanks for the Cap and Trade
Our gas prices will rise
Right before our eyes
Coal industry he'll bankrupt-ee
B.O. won't compromise
We Thank you, so much.

Thanks for your honesty
You promised you'd be fair
Filled with savoir faire
But all we see are Tax Cheat-ees
Transparency's not there
We thank you so much.

Many are the things that you promised
You said you'd cut out ear-marks, but honest!
A trillion dollar bail-out's upon us
It's Spending-gate,
And Crisis-State!

So, Thanks for the Wagyu Beef
And parties every week,
Telelprompter-speak
We changed for hope
But we were dopes
And in remorse We Weep!
But, Thank you, so much.

And Thanks for Dear Hillary
In doo doo she has stepped
With Buttons called 'Reset'
But silly she, her translate-ee
Was blonde and not brunette
We Thank you so much.

And when Gordon Brown came to visit
And brought along some gifts quite exquisite
A present of some movies don't get it!
Now ain't that class?
B.O.'s an ass

Thanks for the GITMO plan Our enemies are thrilled
Beans they now have spilled
It seems they knew that he'd come through
So now their plans re-build
We thank you so much.

Anyone who thinks he was hoping
For regular Joes to triumph is joking
I don't know what the stuff is you're smoking
But, Marxist thought is what we bought

So, Thanks for our crushing debt
Our grandchildren will wish
They could escape the ditch
But what the hell You're looking swell
Your parties fever-pitch
We thank you, so much.

And....thanks to the Democrats
and all you other folks
For voting in this Joke
In four short years, we'll be in tears
Because we'll all be broke..
Although you thought that hope would float
his guy ain't Ivory Soap
So, thank you!
So Much

Chapter Two:
Political Hot Buttons

Lib'ruls

There is a certain satisfaction from doing this parody based on the song made famous by one of the most famous liberals in Hollywood. So here is People, original Music by Jule Styne. Lyrics by Bob Merril. I hope that Babs likes it.

Lib'ruls! People who are Lib'ruls
Are the silliest people in the world,
They're children, whining crying children
Never trying to be adult
They'd rather pout and sulk
Acting just like numbskulls
Those Lib'ruls.

Lib'ruls are just emoting people,
They think all the world's problems started here
Then they tell you, the solution is to tax you,
Just see your paycheck and laugh
Once it was whole
Now it's half.
You may hunger and thirst
But first
Pay the government your taxes
They'll just ignore the fact is
They fund the stupidest programs
In the world!

They'll tell you brother,
Why don't you share with others?
Just see your paycheck and laugh
Once it was whole
Now it's half.
For whatever it's worth
No mirth
To be found among the Lib'ruls

Oh those silly Lib'ruls
Funding all their pet programs
With Our Dough!

LIBS!
Kids! from Bye Bye Birdie [Note: BDS =Bush Derangement Syndrome]

Libs!
I don't know what's wrong with these libs today!
Libs!
Why should we believe anything they say?
Libs!
They've got a bone to pick, fraught with BDS!
Angry, crazy, snarky, lazy, Loafers!
While we're on the subject:
Libs!
You can talk and talk till your face is blue!
Libs!
But they still won't do what you ask them to!
Why can't they be like we are
Perfect in every way?
What's the matter with Libs today?

Libs!
Big Nanny Staters and hypocrites!
Libs! Libs!
Shameless, Hustling, Lying, Spinning Morons!
And while we're on the subject!
Libs!
They are just impossible to control!
Libs!
With their congressmen and now old B.O.!
Why can't they see it our way?
Won't they turn Right we say!
What's the matter with Libs today?

Liberals in the Dark

Chicago made a hit with "Saturday in the Park." This was written at the request of my friend, Curtal Friar. Original artists Chicago (Robert Lamm). This was written in April 2008 when there was a dead heat between Barack Obama and Hillary Clinton for the Democratic Nomination.

Liberals in the dark
I think they hate the fourth of July
Liberals in the dark
I think they hate the fourth of July
Freedom leaching, over-reaching
A PAC selling favors
So much they know is wrong
Global warming, Al Gore warning
Oil? Won't dig it (but we should)
We've been wasting such a long time
For a new day.

Campaign trail, What's that say?
You'd think we'd all roll over and die
RINO pol, John McCain
And Hilly and BO are a tie
Talking Health care, really lying
They all sing the same song
Shilling for us all
Will you help them change the world?
I don't dig it (no, I don't)
'cause we're all waiting for a new Prez
Just to blame

I wish we'd tell them "Fly red, white and blue today"
The MSM still can spin stories their own way
Listen children just weigh the cost, just weigh the cost!

Everyday fight the dark
Hold onto the fourth of July
Knock the Dems, out the Park
Hold onto the fourth of July
People teaching, people touching
And our Soldiers fighting
Protecting us all
If we want it, really want it
Can you dig it (yes, I can)
Don't go waiting such a long time
Seize the day!

Tellin' Ya Lies!
From Saturday Night Fever, 'Stayin' Alive'
(Bee Gees) with the Obama twist.

Well, you can tell by the way I walk the walk
I'm a lyin' man each time I talk
When I told you, you'd be informed,
It's a trick, and now
You have been warned
But now its all right, its okay
Just go look the other way
Don't you try to understand
Obamanation's in my hand

Whether your a brother or whether your a mother
I'm tellin' a lie, tellin' a lie
Feel the White House shakin' and all your taxes takin'
I'm tellin' a lie, tellin' a lie
Ah, ha ha ha, tellin' a lie, tellin' a lie
Ah ha ha ha tellin' a lie!

Well now, polls are low and then they're high
It don't matter which, 'cause I really try
My name is always in the news
I'm Obama man, and I just can't lose
I hear from the Right, it's okay
I'm glib, I'll see another day
Don't you try to understand
The New Regime's Obamaland!

Whether you're a brother or whether you're a mother
I'm tellin' ya lies, tellin' ya lies
See I've got a 'stake' in the country that I'm takin'
I'm tellin' ya lies, tellin' ya lies
Ah ha ha ha tellin' ya lies, tellin' ya lies
Ah ha ha ha tellin' ya lies!

Right's goin' nowhere, those newsguys help me
Those newsguys help me, yeah.
Right's goin' nowhere,
the Congress helps me
the Congress helps me, yeah,
tellin' ya lies!

Well, you can tell by the way I walk the walk
I'm a lyin' man each time I talk
When I told you, you'd be informed,
It's a trick, and now
You have been warned
But now its all right, its okay
Just go look the other way
Don't you try to understand
Obamanation's in your land

Whether you're a brother or whether you're a mother
I'm tellin' ya lies, tellin' ya lies
See I've got a 'stake' in the country that I'm takin'
I'm tellin' ya lies, tellin' ya lies
Ah ha ha ha tellin' ya lies, tellin' ya lies
Ah ha ha ha tellin' ya lies!

Lies goin' out there, MSM helps me
MSM helps me, yeah.
Lies goin' out there, the congress helps me, yeah
We're tellin' ya lies!

The Night the Lights Went Out in Congress

Vicki Lawrence and Reba McIntire have made hits with the song, "That's the Night that the Lights Went Out in Georgia" Here's a remix to reflect the brave and honorable folks that refused to leave the House, even though Nancy Pelosi shut out the lights. Sorry for the little Hip Hop Lingo.
Bobby Russell 'The Night the Lights Went out In Georgia'

They were on their way to a juggernaut
Repubs were on and she thought they'd stop!
Celebs like Nancy don't think they should listen to them

Nancy, solo, she said Woah
We said why? What you doin' Ho?
Nan said sit down, I got some bad news that's gonna hurt.

Said I'm the queen bee, and you know that's right
But I'm not stayin' or I'll miss my flight
Since I'm not wrong, don't matter what you think should be said

They got mad and they saw red
Pelosi said fine, you can all drop dead
Then she turned off the lights, the mikes and cameras and fled.

That's the night that the lights went off in Congress
That's the night that they stopped our energy plan
Don't trust our oil to no backwards speaker Nancy
Cause the Dems in that town are lamebrains just like Nan

Nancy went off on her new book tour
Skipping out of town just to spread her manure
You see, Nancy doesn't have any cred and she thinks we are blind

Honor-bound guys, they didn't leave town
Stayed on the floor and finally found
The only thing they have been lacking and that is a spine!

They are staying there in the House
Working out some plans in spite of P-louse
Just holding the line 'til Ten Senators came

We all wish they'd even the score
That Gang of Ten we've seen before
Crossing the aisle, compromising their name

Those Patriot men were standing their ground
When those Ten showed up just to shoot 'em down
And a big hearted voter grabbed his head and said
"Why'd you do it?"

We say they're guilty of a make-believe style
Slapping the voters with a puny stockpile and say
Voters prices are high and you'd best get used to it

That's the night that the lights went off in Congress
That's the night that the Dems rejected our plan
Don't trust our soil to no backwards speaker Nancy
Cause the Dems in that town are lamebrains just like Nan

They stung those others before they could say
To stand our ground was a better way
To get more oil, in fact our side defines!

And those cheatin' Dems that had to leave town
That's one body that 'll have to go down
You see all us voters don't miss all the mischief they've done

That's the night that the lights went off in Congress
That's the night that she stopped our energy plan
Don't trust our soil to no backwards speaker Nancy
Cause the Dems in that town are lamebrains just like Nan

That's the night that the lights went out in Congress
That's the night that Pelosi thwarted our plan
Well don't trust our Oil to no backwards lefty party
Cause the Dems in that town are lamebrains just like Nan.

When Congress is in Session
To the refrain/tune "When Irish Eyes are Smiling"
(Chauncey Olcott/George Graff, Jr.)

When Congress is in session
Sure it's like the Borg on earth
Saying we'll be 'stimulated'
While they latch on to our purse

When B. Hussein's not happy
It's on Rush he blames the play
For when B. Hussein's not smiling
Soon he'll steal our voice away.

When Nancy sounds beguiling
Sure, 'tis like a plague indeed
Hang her guilty from the rafters
In an effigy with Reid

When Barney Frank is talking
Sure the lisp is hard to bear
But when lights are on them shining
We can see that there's no 'there' there!

When banks are downhill sliding
Sure it sounds like FDR
Like a cavalry they're riding
All I see are commissars

When Congressmen and Senate
Take no blame for what they've done
That's when we must start up-rising
Lest they soon steal away our guns

The 110th Congress
To the tune of There's a Yellow Rose in Texas.

There's some Democrats in Congress,
One name is Harry Reid
Nobody else can top him
In thought or word or deed
He tries to sound like Churchill,
But troop funds he denies
And if he's re-elected, who will apologize?

He's the biggest little whiner
That Congress ever knew
He says he'll back the troops but
He hasn't got a clue
You may talk about Ted Kennedy
Or scream at Nancy P.
But all Democrats in Congress are a travesty to me.

When you think about the danger
If Nancy were the Prez
You'd know we need to stop them
They hang out with Chavez
We must change the tone, and find a way
To stop these bureaucrats
No more Tax and Spend Republicans! Let's squash the Democrats!

They're the biggest little losers
That Congress ever saw
If gridlock were in fashion,
They'd win for shock and awe
They'd hand out more perks to Immigrants
Who aren't here legally
For the Hundred and tenth Congress is a shame from sea to sea.

When the Democrats are talking
They try to sound so bright
They say they'll raise our taxes,
Or the Patriot Act's a blight
They'll withhold the funds from soldiers
Or say the war is lost
They only help Al Qaeda, no matter what the cost.

They're the biggest bunch of losers
That Congress ever knew
Their scandals include Clinton
Who gets her funds from Hsu
You may think they care about this land
But observations tell
That the Hundred and Tenth Congress is so low it rests in hell.

Those Pols are Deranged
Based on Home on the Range by Brewster Higley and Daniel Kelley. Visitors to my blog reminded me that the original is the Kansas State Song.

How often those pols try to inflate their roles
Never true to constituent's minds
I have stood there amazed and asked as I gazed
Can this tangle we ever unwind?

Gone, Gone are the days
Where the Dems and Republicans play
Now seldom is heard a cooperative word
And the skies are just gloomy all day

Which party will lead? Anyone our voice heed?
Can they do what we sent them to do?
Uphold our great land, with a miserly hand
But they've both failed; the Red and the Blue!

When, when will they see?
That the Congress should hear you and me?
Where seldom is heard our most critical words
And the pols just say 'Re-elect me!'

Oh give me a tome, where economists hone
Sound advice, every principle state
Send it to the swamp where it smells like de-comp
So they'll learn a free market is great

Why, Why can't they learn?
When we sent them to their Congress term
We wanted their voice to enable our choice
Not be raised to campaign at mid-term

Once this land was true to the Founders' breakthrough
Where our freedoms were held up as good
And now we have pols with elitism goals
Telling us what to think, what to do!

They all are deranged!
When they tell us our goal must be changed
Why can't they just stop all of this agitprop?
And allow us our freedom again?

Most Writers Spin His Lies
Johnny Cash and the movie "City Slickers," made this famous.
"Ghost Riders in the Sky" by Stan Jones

As I was reading 'bout the Presidential race today
I looked upon the written words my attitude to sway
When all at once I surely heard my inner voice rebel
To glowing words Obama spoke, and what reporters tell

Their hands and voice admire him, they magnify his spiel
And tingling leg excitement pegs the bias that they feel
A bolt of fear went through me as I listened to this guy
For he saw Obama coming hard, and began to spread his lies

Yippie Yi Ohhhhhh!
Yippie Yi Yaaaaay!
Most Writers Spin His Lies

The race is run, McCain is done, they're sure to poke that vet
Quote Wesley Clark, believe that shark,
but John ain't fought him yet
'Cause they're bound to spin it their way,
they embrace Change from that guy
Not seeing he's a liar
As they write on hear me sigh.

As the writers hype Obama I heard someone call my name
If you want to save your soul from Hell a-sliding into Change
Then voter change your ways today or with us you will die
Listening to Obama's word, embracing endless lies.

Yippie Yi Yaaaaay!
Yippie Yi Ohhhh!
Most writers spin his Lies
Most Writers Spin His Lies
(Repeat & Fade)

Oh I'm Snarling
To the tune of My Darling Clementine, by Barker Bradford 1885.
There are a lot of verses to this tune. Here's another permutation.

At the Congress, aim a cannon
Aiming just to change their minds
It's not minor, They're all whiners
Drilling now would buy us time

Chorus: Oh, I'm snarling, Oh, I'm snarling,
Oh, I'm snarling all the time
All is Lost! Vote for Dems? Never!
'Cause I think they're asinine!

We need miners, no more whiners
Don't you wish we'd oil refine?
But the Congress makes no progress
They're experts at monkeyshines.
Chorus
Like the voters that want Barry
(And he's less than forty-nine!)
Most are youthful but be truthful
Education's in decline.
Chorus
Talking lightly, that is Barry
Teleprompters help him shine
Sometimes tripping, Then he's flipping
And he doesn't have a spine!
Chorus
In a Church, harsh as it sounded
Reverend Wright made an opine
Blames the White Folks, Hate unbounded
And all ills to them assigns
Chorus
If we just had someone better
Than McCain, I wouldn't mind
Dont you wish a clue he'd get here?

But at least he has a spine.
Chorus
No Dems want another Kerry
So they just ignore the signs
Marxist Lefty is their Barry
But he'll make the finish-line
Chorus
When we've chosen the next POTUS
Don't you wish we had a choice?
It's a Geezer, or Bull-Squeezer
Gosh, I think I've lost my voice.

Oh, I'm snarling, Oh, I'm snarling,
Oh, I'm snarling all the time
No Big Gov'ment, No Incumbents!
Our Republic's on the line.

Drunken Sailors!

This was written by request from GunnyG upon his return from Iraq. My little way of saying "Welcome Home!" It points out the flagrant abuse by the Politicians in Washington spending taxpayers' money like (wait for it) Drunken Sailors! Based on a sea chantey.

What shall we do with the drunken sailors?
What shall we do with the drunken sailors?
What shall we do with the drunken sailors?
Vote them out of office!

[Chorus]
Way hay elect some misers
Way hay elect some misers
Way hay elect some misers
Read our Constitution!

Listen to the sound; see my finger waggin'
Listen to the sound; see my finger waggin'
Listen to the sound; Mrs. Paddy's raggin'
Stop those Drunken Sailors!

(Chorus)

Hold them to account for their wasteful spending
Hold them to account for their wasteful spending
Hold them to account for their wasteful spending
Taxes have a limit!

(Chorus)

Stop *quid pro quo* and tax and spending
Stop *quid pro quo* and tax and spending
Stop *quid pro quo* and tax and spending
Balance now the budget!

(Chorus)

What should we do with the drunken sailors?
What should we do with the drunken sailors?
What should we do with the drunken sailors?
Kick them out, NO WARNING!

(Chorus)

Save our nation with a vote for freedom
Save our nation with a vote for freedom
Save our nation with a vote for freedom
Free from Drunken Sailors!!

Way hay elect some misers
Way hay elect some misers
Se-lect some who're wise to
Heed our Constitution!

Porkbusters

CAGW is doing good work, and here's a song to go along with the fight against pork in Washington! From Ghostbusters, the theme written by Ray Parker Jr.

If you're sick and tired,
Of the Congress Pork
Who you gonna call?
(Porkbusters)
They're from every state,
Even from New York
Who you gonna call?
(Porkbusters)

All those liars are toast
All those liars are toast

If those Congressmen.
Keep on Wasting Dough
Who can you call?
(Porkbusters)

Ain't it all a sham,
Keeping voters dumb
Oh, who you gonna call?
(Porkbusters)

All those liars are toast
All those liars are toast

Who you gonna call
(Porkbusters)
Believe a word I spoke?
Get out and Vote
And BE
Porkbusters!

All those liars are toast
I hear they think we're scum
All those liars are toast
Yeah, yeah, yeah, yeah

Who you gonna call?
(Porkbusters)

If you've had enough,
Then we must be tough
Then we all can be:
Porkbusters!

Let me tell you something
Bustin' makes me feel good

All those liars are toast
All those liars are toast

Don't think you're alone,
Oh no
Porkbusters
Ah, I think we better all be
Porkbusters!

Send them all out the door
Unless you just want some more

Ee I Ee I Ouch!
From the children's song: Old MacDonald's Farm

The Senators and Congress, Oh!
Ee I Ee I Ouch!
They like to spend taxpayers' dough!
Ee I Ee I Ouch!
With some pork-pork here,
And more pork-pork there,
Voters squeal, please repeal
Every mother's son feels
Congressmen have got to go
Ee I Ee I Ouch!

When to the Swamp they were elect
Ee I Ee I Ouch!
They all claimed to be circumspect
Ee I Ee I Ouch!
But there's more pork here
And some scandal there
Tax and spend, without end
Don't you want to stop them?
Congressmen our voice reject.
Ee I Ee I Ouch!

One day citizens will rise
Ee I Ee I Ouch!
We'll see them with wide open eyes
Ee I Ee I Ouch!
Then we'll vote reform
Tell them they are warned
Drive them out, with a shout
We have had our fill about
Congressmen who are not wise
Ee I Ee I Ouch!

Sixteen Tons of Pork!
From the classic country song by Tennessee Ernie Ford, "Sixteen Tons"

We sent you all to Congress in the hope you would shine
You got there to Washington but didn't toe the line
We need you to keep our sovereignty
No more violence to our liberty

Chorus: You load pork on top of every last bill
If you don't get the picture then my vote you ne'er will
Campaigners don't you call me 'cause I can't go
I will not vote for another RINO

Well, if you can't spend responsibly then step aside
Your RINO ways we cannot abide
Tax and spend, your conscience weak
Reform today or you'll lose your seat.

(Chorus)

We don't want big brother and we don't want healthcare
Those socialist programs never go anywhere
We want some reform, tax cuts for good
Won't you just do what you know you should?

(Chorus)

If you want to stay in office then our voice you should hear
We don't want illegals to remain over here
We need the fence and to enforce the law
Ignoring that is the very last straw.

(Chorus)

Don't ya tell me brother that we need the UN
That scandal shack has never been our friend

As far as Kyoto and LOST - They're lies
Don't continue to close your ears and your eyes
(*Chorus*)

With November comin' better think some more
We sent you in to watch over the store
Come election day our wrath will rise
We're tellin' you now we've had our fill of your lies
(*Chorus*)

Give Back!
From the Beatles' hit "Get Back"

Joe Blow was a man who thought he was a winner
But he knew it wouldn't last
Joe Blow had a thought his wallet would be thinner
Congress called him middle-class

Give Back, give back.
Give back to Congress what you owe
Give Back, give back
The Congress wants to spend your dough
Give back Joe Blow. Your Dough.
Give Back, give back
Give back to Congress what you owe
Give back Joe.

Money-maker Molly wants to keep her earnings
But the taxman weighs the score
All the IRS will say's they've got it coming
And they'll get it all and more

Give back, give back
Give back and let the Congress score
Give back, give back
Give back or face solicitor
Give back, give back
Give back we are your Senators
Give back, give back
Give or see our auditor
Give back Money-maker!

The Congress's waiting for you
Waiting to spend your dough
From their fur-lined pockets
Re-election is here

Give back, give back.
Give back and let the Congress score

Take the Money You Bums
Steve Miller "Take the Money and Run" (which works too!)

This here's a story about Harry Reid and Nancy too
Two of them in Congress with nothin' better to do
Than flit about the "House," just work when in the mood
And here is what happened when Barry told 'em 'Cut Loose"
They doubled down to, ooh, end the crisis!
Enacting their plans as if it were stare decisis
Drunken sailors worse than old Dionysus

They all took our money, the bums
They all took our money, the bums
They all took our money, the bums
They all took our money, the bums
They all took our money, the bums

Barry's tactic is to blame that guy in Texas
You know he knows just exacly what the facts is
He ain't gonna take the blame for when he was in Congress
No matter he promised us to lower our taxes
Campaign promises? Whoa, they've slipped away
The course we're heading down just changes day to day
They got the money hey
They think they've saved the day
Th'economy's down but there's still more for them to slay
Singin'
We all took your money, we won!
We all took your money, we won!
We all took your money, we won!
(repeat & fade)

Look Out for Mr. Tax
From the movie, Dumbo
"Look Out for Mr. Stork" by Churchill & Washington

Look out for Mr. Tax
That persevering chap
He'll come along and steal
That bundle from your lap
You may be poor or rich
It doesn't matter which
Millionaires, they lose theirs
Like the butcher and the baker
So look out for Mr. Tax
And let me tell you, friend
Don't try to get away
He'll find you in the end
The IRS will nail you And they will not even ask
So you better look out for Mr. Tax.

Look out for Mr. Tax
He's got you on his list
And when he comes around
It's useless to resist
Remember Wesley Snipes's in jail
and don't you know it's true
The tax man has his eye on you!

Angst for the Centuries
From the old Bob Hope classic song, "Thanks for the Memories"
Original song by Leo Robin and Ralph Rainger.

Angst for the Centuries
Of things we can't undo
Don't you know it's true?
Our Democrats and Bureaucrats
Republicrats screw you
How hopeless it is

Angst for the centuries
And how could we forget
Nan Pelosi's jet?
Those junket trips and those loose lips
How craven can they get?
How foolish they are!

(*Chorus*)
Now with this campaign I'm madder
It all seems to point to disaster
How sad we'll all be morning-after
Who is the chump? We bought their stump.

But, angst for the centuries
Is certain to prevail
Don't social programs fail?
But what to do, the joke's on you
Your check is in the mail
They thank you so much!

Angst for the centuries
We're bitter now it's true
Neither red nor blue
We had a choice, but lost our voice
And now it seems we're screwed
How awful it is!

Angst for the memories
Of documents destroyed
Pay-offs they enjoyed
They all are sharks, with more ear-marks
Why should they be employed?
How crooked they are!

(*Chorus*)

Now that we see the election
Is giving the folks no selection
If only we'd voice our objection
And start again
They're no ones friend

So Angst for the Centuries
Is all we have to cheer
Socialism's here
We had a vote, but now we'll choke
On all we have to fear
And it scares me, so much!

Wreck of the G.O.P.
Gordon Lightfoot's 'Edmund Fitzgerald'

A legend lives on from the Chippewa on down
Of a party once called the G.O.P.
No conservatives led, in fact we think it's dead
Now the skies of November are gloomy

It started to wane when they chose John McCain
His conservative claims are all empty
His amnesty fight will not make it all right
When the polls of November came early

Ron Reagan showed pride in the American side
And the G.O.P. brand was so pleasin'
With his military pride and respect far and wide
Grand old Party was now in its season

But what did they do when they bested the blue?
When they had both the House and the Senate?
They squandered our dough and they failed to oppose
Every Democrat's awful agenda.

Dubya failed then to wield his veto pen
The agenda of growth was in season
Instead of a stand he just jumped to the band
And the G.O.P. lost rhyme and reason

McCain dipped his quill into the Feingold bill
Good intentions have led us to ruin
Instead of free speech no incumbents we'll breach
And the MSM now leads the shoe-in

Does anyone know where the rule of law goes
When the illegal aliens are harbored?
No border defense, nor have they built up the fence
And McCain is no longer to starboard

We might have had Mitt, Hunter, Rudy or Huck
If the powers that be were not clueless
But all that remain are the faces and names
Of the ones who are left and they're useless!

The legend lives on from the Chippewa on down
Of a party once called the G.O.P.
It abandoned its base and will now lose the race
Now the gales of November came early.

Oh Yes! We're the Great Pretenders
*No surprise, I was not happy with any of the front-runners for President, and haven't been since this parody was written in mid-January 2008. This fits every candidate, regardless of party.
'The Great Pretender,' Freddie Mercury/The Platters.*

Oh yes, I'm the great pretender (ooh ooh)
Pretending I will be your Prez (ooh ooh)
I want your vote, Your ideals I'll float
I'm lying but no one can tell

Oh yes, I'm the great pretender (ooh ooh)
Adrift in my pandering campaign (ooh ooh)
I play the game; MSM's to blame
For making my words sound so lame

It's real that you think it's all make believe
It's real when you hear and my words cause you fear

Ooh Ooh Yes they're the great pretenders (ooh ooh)
Believing that voters are clowns (ooh ooh)
They seem to be what they're not (you see)
They'll trample our heart for the crown
Pretending that they're White House bound

Yeah Ooh Hoo
It's real when you hear and their voice causes fear

Oh Yes We're the great pretenders
Just voting for those we don't like (ooh ooh)
They seem to be what they're not you see
Why can't we find someone to trust?
Pretending we don't feel disgust

Flip Flop!
Everybody, it seems, has made a recording of this song: Bobby Darin, Little Richard and even Barbra Streisand! So, based on "Splish Splash"...I think you see the candidate it features.

Flip Flop, all his statements he'll swap
Won't you watch him move to the right?
Flub dub changing angles, that's the rub
Don't you wish he'd be more forthright?

Well he stepped on a nerve
Asked "what're patriots for?"
Then wrapped the flag around him
Spun it all like Mike Moore
And then Flip Flop
It's not a malaprop
Well don't you know for sure that the election's goin' on?

He's just a flippin' and a floppin'
Feelin' more appealin'
Provin' he's a movin'
Mockin' all the pollin'
Hey, Yeah!

Ding Dong I saw he was wrong
When he said he knew Reverend Wright
Yeah, flip flop credibility dropped
When he said his friends were all right

There was Rezko and Pfleger, Bill Ayers was there too
What folly all his friends are worse than Hillary's Hsu!
Well Flip Flop forget that agitprop
He went and pulled the switcheroo off, yeah!

He is lying and a whining
Wheelin' and a dealin'
Newsy he will schmmozy

Flippin' and a Floppin'
Yeah!

Yeah, he is a flippin' and a floppin'
He's just a wheelin' and a dealin'
Yeah! In the news he is a schmooz-er
He's feelin' he's appealin'
But is he dopin' and a smokin'?
Lyin' and a whinin'?
Flip Flop, Yeah!

Flippin' and a Floppin'
This time he's dashin' but he's crashin'
He's just a rollin' with the pollin'
Yeah! He is a flippin' and a floppin'

It's A Zoo
From Simon and Garfunkle's "At the Zoo"

Someone told me
All the candidates lie to you
I do believe it
I do believe it's true

OO OO OO
MMM MMM MMM MMM MMM
Oh Oh Oh Oh Oh
OO OO OO OO OO

It's a rough and tumble journey
Once they take to their campaign
Just a bold expensive gamble
To get you

To get the vote they'll lie to us
Til they're gaining, It gets old
And the candidates will love it
If you do
If you do now

Something tells me
All the candidates lie to you

Where do we look for honesty
They all are insincere
And the elephants are RINOs and that's dumb
Obama says he's skeptical
Of why the war still rages
And the Oprah says she's there to help him run

Liberals are reactionaries
Huckabee's a 'missionary'
Clintons plot in secrecy

And voters turn off frequently
What a gas!
You gotta realize
It's a Zoo!
It's a Zoo!
(*Repeat and fade*)

Getting to Know Them
From the King and I, "Getting to Know you" (Rodgers & Hammerstein)

It's a very ancient saying
But a true and honest thought
That if you run for office
By your statements you'll be caught
As a voter I've been learning
(You'll forgive me if I choke)
And I've now become an expert,
On the subject: How to Vote
[*spoken*]
Getting to know Them
[*voters giggle*]
Getting to know Them,
Getting to know all about them
Nothing to like when
Nobody else speaks for me

Getting to know them, seeing it my way
Precisely,
Putting it 'nicely'
Don't muck with me
[*voters giggle*]

Getting to know them
Getting to know all about them
Nothing to like when
Nobody else speaks for me
Getting to know them, seeing it my way
Precisely,
Putting it nicely
Don't muck with me

Getting to know them
Wanting to feel free, that's easy!
And so I listen

Getting to know how they play
Haven't you noticed
Obama's bright but sleazy?
Because of all those character-flawed friends
Do the means justify ends?
No! I Say!

Getting to know them
Wishing away John, that's easy
But though his older
Don't you believe what he says?
Haven't you noticed?
Life isn't easy-peasy
I don't believe he's as evil as B.O.
Use your Audacity to vote!
No! B. O.!

Pop! Pols are Weasels

Frustrated with candidates that ignore the voice of 'we the people,' I wrote the following based on the children's song: Pop Goes the Weasel. I was particularly annoyed by the remark by Nancy Pelosi regarding the Democrats' decision not to count the delegates in Michigan and Florida (which they later half-reversed). When she referred to the delegates and electoral process as 'Coin of the Realm' she revealed the politicians in Washington, DC carry an attitude more of royalty than the public servants they are. I think all incumbents should be removed from office.

Around and round they all insult Bush
Obama and the Geezer
The voters think it's all in fun
Pop! Pols are weasels!

A penny for a subsidy
More money for their coffers
That's the way the money goes!
Pop! Pols are weasels!

A fifty bill to fill up my tank
More ethanol is silly
Attack Big Oil and say it's a vice
Pop! Pols are weasels!

Up and down the campaign road
But whose votes will be counted?
Nancy says just 'coin of the realm'
Pop! Pols are weasels!

With Greenies I've a thing to remark
Your laws make us pay double
We need to drill and nuclearize
Pop! Pols are Weasels!

I've no time to plead and pine
With voters I'll not wheedle
Kick them out 'til there are none!
Pop! Pols are Weasels!

Wake Up, Smell the Coffee!
The Everly Brothers had a hit with 'Wake Up Little Susie" Felice and Boudleaux Bryant

Wake up, smell the coffee, wake up!
Wake up, smell the coffee, wake up!
The candidates we seek
Aren't the best we've got they are weak
The campaign's over, it's down the drain
And we're in trouble deep
Wake up, smell the coffee
Wake up, smell the coffee

Well...
Why are we gonna vote for Obama?
What is the appeal of McCain?
What are we gonna do, will we all just bend o'er again?
Wake up, smell the coffee!
Wake up, smell the coffee!

Well I see Obama has made a gaffe again
Well Democrats looks like you goofed again
Wake up, smell the coffee!
Wake up, smell the coffee!
Just send him on home

Wake up, smell the coffee, wake up!
Wake up, smell the coffee, wake up!
John McCain isn't so hot
But looks like he's the best that we've got
No border fence, our goose is cooked
Our sovereign nation is shot
Wake up, smell the coffee!
Wake up, smell the coffee!

Well...
Why are we gonna vote for Obama?
What is the appeal of McCain?
What are we gonna do, will we all just bend o'er again?
Wake up, smell the coffee!
Wake up, smell the coffee!

Dubya Said He'd Change the Tone
The Temptations, "Papa Was a Rolling Stone"
Norm Whitfield & Barrett Strong

It was the 4th of November
That day I'll always remember, yes I will
Cause that was the day our republic died
We never got a chance to cheer him - Never
hear nothing but bad things about him
And now, why don't you listen to me while I tell you the truth

(Chorus)
Dubya said he'd change the tone
Whenever he came into Washington
(But when he tried)
All they left him was alone."
Dubya said he'd change the tone
Whenever he came into Washington
(But when he tried)
All they left him was alone.

Well, well.....
Hey Congress, is it true what they say,
That hanging chads held up the election for two months?
And Congress, some bad talk going around town
Saying that Dubya stole the election in the Al Gore fight
And that ain't right.
They, talk about Dubya doing drugs and drive drinkin'
Congress said they'd cooperate and all the time winkin'
Dealing in lies, and blaming Mr. Bush for it all.

(Chorus)

Tell me how George Bush won a second election?
Folks said he'd trample rights just to give us protection
But is there anyone there to tell us the truth?
And Congress? They say that Dubya never was much on thinking

Waste money and time; their approval is sinking.
But we'll not be depending on them to tell us the truth.

"Sons, Dubya said he'd change the tone (well, well, well, well)
Whenever he came into Washington
(But when he tried)
All they left him was alone. Lone, lone, lone, lone alone"
(Chorus ... Fade)

I'm the Decider
From the Monkees' Hit "I'm a Believer" Neil Diamond

We thought we could always hide from terrorists
They'd hurt someone else but never we
They set out to get us
And on Nine One One
O. bin Laden shattered all our dreams

Then Bush took him on, said, "I'm the decider"
No one saw a doubt in his mind
He is strong, He's the decider
Not a backslider, strong of spine!

Now we face another choice for President
Seems when we need choice the less we get
We don't want more RINOs
All they give is pain
We just want Conservatives again!

Now then when I can vote, I'm the Decider!
No one sees a doubt in my mind
When I vote, I'm the Decider
No more backsliders, strong of spine!

Repeat chorus

Now when you vote, You're the Decider!
Inform your choice, no doubts in your mind
When you vote, You're the Decider
No more a backslider, Qualified!

Rock the Vote

This was an idea inspired by YLG.
From Hues Corporation's Number One Hit "Rock the Boat"

So we'd like to show that, we have the motion
So we'd like to show that, we have the notion

To rock the vote, we'll rock the vote baby
Rock the vote, we'll tip the Dems over
Rock the vote, we'll rock the vote baby
Rock the Vo-oh-oh-oh-ote!

Ever since our love of USA began
We've sought to keep this strong and prosperous land
She has been a beacon from sea to shining sea
Our strength is in our nation that will set you free
At stake is our freedom and prosperity
Come along and find a candidate that, upholds liberty!

So we'd like to show that, we have the motion
So we'd like to show that, we have the notion

To rock the vote, we'll rock the vote baby
Rock the vote, we'll tip the Dems over
Rock the vote, we'll rock the vote baby
Rock the Vo-oh-oh-oh-ote!

Our ship of state has sailed through every storm
And we want someone who'll keep her safe from harm
Oh we need to keep her strong and bold and free
Elect someone who will not tax us into poverty!

So we'd like to show that, we have the motion
So we'd like to show that, we have the notion

To rock the vote, we'll rock the vote baby
Rock the vote, we'll tip the Dems over
Rock the vote, we'll rock the vote baby
Rock the Vo-oh-oh-oh-ote!

Vote the G O P
*Crosby, Stills, Nash and Young's "Love the One
You're With" original lyrics: Will Young*

If you're down and confused
And you think nobody
Will represent you
Constitution slips away
Cos your values seem passe today

But there's some hope in our native land
Where the eagle flies at our command
And if you can't vote for the one you love, honey
Vote the G O P

Don't be angry, don't be sad
Don't sit crying over good times we had
There's a cause, much bigger than you
To help our nation is what we should do

Cos there's some hope in our native land
And the eagle flies to our command
And if you can't vote for the one you love, honey
Vote the G O P

Turn from heartache; embrace some joy
The Constitution, we'll employ
Don't skip the election, it's your voice
And you don't need to give up your choice

Cos there's some hope in freedom's land
And our eagle flies, Take a stand!
But if you can't vote for the one you love, honey
Vote the G O P

Vote for You and Me
Vote the G O P
Do do do do do do doo, do do do do do do doo
Do do do do do do do do, do-do-do, do-do-do!

Stop! It's Election Day!
*From the Supremes'
'Stop! In the Name of Love" by Brian Holland/
Lamont Dozier/Edward Holland, Jr.*

Maybe, maybe
We can turn the tide of change
If we just hold the course
We must keep our intentions clear
Our Constitution and our Values near

But this time before we cast our vote
Wond'ring if we can rock the boat
(think it over)
Will our candidate be strong?
(Think it over)
Will it be our nation's swan song?

(*Chorus*)
Stop! It's election day
Don't keep yourself away
Stop! It's election day
Don't keep yourself away
Think it over
Think it over

I've watched the polls
Polls that say we've lost
I've even seen them
Calculate the cost
But has the MSM's affection
Guaranteed they'll sway this election?
But this time before you stay at home
Please listen to this poem
(think it over) Do we want Obama Prez?
(Think it over)
Do we want our own Chavez?

(Chorus)

I've tried so hard to fight disinformation
Hoping we'd stop this abomination
But with one voice the MSM's together
And I'm afraid this storm we cannot weather
(Chorus)

Gov Train

More and more I see the USA creeping toward socialism instead of freedom. With the current crop of politicians, especially the Presidential Candidates, I don't feel like I have a voice either. So here's one from the O'Jays' "Love Train." This train's name is Big Government.

People in the USA (everybody)
Join hands (join)
Hop the Gov Train, Gov Train
People all over the land (Just like the world now)
Join Hands
Hop the Gov Train, Gov Train
You know how we tried to break from England
We'll be like the folks in Russia, and China too
Don't you know it's past time we were onboard
Cause this train keeps on riding, riding on through
Well, Well

All you Candidates
Join Hands
Start the Gov Train, Gov Train
Just like all over the world
Join In
Run that Gov Train, Gov Train

Obama has some brothers over in Africa
He'll send them money but hands off Israel, too
Don't you know that this train's in our nation
And if you diss it, I feel sorry, sorry for you
Well

People all over the world
Comrade
Love the Gov Train, Gov Train
People all over the world
They live
Under a Gov Train, Gov Train

Ride, Let it ride
Don't you try
To stem the tide!

People all over the world
Join in
Lose your freedoms, Gov Train
People all over the world
Give in
Trust the Gov Train, Gov Train
Socialize (come on)
Take the Gov Train, Gov Train

Send Them Back, Jack
From Steely Dan's "Do It Again" Here is a little song about Illegal Aliens

In the morning they go running '
'Cross the US southern border
And patrolmen can not fire
'Cause they haven't got no order
And illegals take our IDs
'Cause they want to steal our nation
And the highways aren't safer
With illegal infiltration
Send them back, Jack, they're not our friends
Illegals 'round 'em up 'round
Send them back, Jack, They're not our friends.

Build a wall and they will climb it,
Or they'll pay to have a guide
Don't enforce the law or border,
Cause they know just where to hide
Those who hire them are evil,
They exploit the poor and yearning
And less honest folk come with them
As we to our doom are learning
Send the back, Jack, they're not our friends

Should al Qaeda have a foot hold,
And they plan to bring us sorrow
All this time we've been ignoring
Consequences for tomorrow
Congress says just let them jump the queue
And they'll be legal voters
We're the land of milk and honey
And we must not close the borders
Send them back, Jack, They're not our friends

No More Silence
From Simon and Garfunkle's, "Sounds of Silence"

Hola! Illegals, you're no friend,
You've come to rob us all again
It's an invasion softly creeping,
Planting seeds while we are sleeping
Reconquista! For the country that you'd gain
Still remains,
Within the sounds of silence

Our border agents walk alone
Facing jail-time from our own
From Lake Tahoe to the border
They cannot shoot without an order
Many folks are stabbed by the thugs from the EME
Called "Emily"
That prowl the streets in silence.

And without Minutemen we saw
A million people maybe more
People talk another language
Working for a hidden slave wage
Singing Spanish songs,
Our Culture never share
And no one dares,
Disturb the Sound of Silence

"Fools" said I "You just don't know,
Amnesty like Cancer grows
Hear my words that I might reach you
Send them home, I need to teach you"
But my words like silent raindrops fell
An no one Dared to Yell
Just Silence

Good folks knelt to sing and pray
Secure our borders now, today!
Won't you stop to heed our warning
Their La Raza now is forming
And their signs say
"The loss of your nation is written if you fail to act!"
Just send them back!
Strong Borders, Rule of Law
No Silence!

PRESSURE

Well, of all the dumb ideas of the past (turn down your thermostat and wear sweaters - Carter) that are being recycled (how green of him!), now Obama states a solution to the energy 'crisis' is to properly inflate your car tires & get a tune up. Well I have a Tune Up for Obama today. From Billy Joel's song, "Pressure!"

You have to learn to save yourself!
PRESSURE
We're worse than everybody else
PRESSURE
I've only had to tout my race, so far
Now you will come to a place
Where the only thing to do
Is heed my words and conserve
Save the Earth with Tire
PRESSURE!
You used to call me Senator
PRESSURE
But soon my voice you won't ignore
PRESSURE
We've turned our nation into Cap and Trade
Now here I am in your face
With my Carteresque advice
Turn down the heat, I repeat
Save the Earth with Tire Pressure!
All dried up, Pelosi's a joke
Hype Sun, Air Too, What does she know?
All your life is Channeling Green
Streets obsolete, what does it mean?
[I'll tell you what it means]
PRESSURE
PRESSURE
Don't ask for help
You're on your own
PRESSURE
Call a tow truck

With your cell phone
PRESSURE
You see I have this comic rationale
And here we are out of oil
And we don't care who we spoil
We've got to drill; gastanks fill
And now I respond with
PRESSURE
PRESSURE
See my wife on Time Magazine
New Yorker too!
What does it mean?
PRESSURE!!!!
I'm sure you'll heed my comic rationale
Just seize my words, put your faith
In my Carteresque advice
Though it's absurd on its face
Just repeat "Watch tire PRESSURE!"
PRESSURE
PRESSURE
One, two, three, four
PRESSURE!!!!!

Come On, It's Just the Weather!
*From the Christmas classic, "Sleigh Ride" by
Leroy Anderson and Mitchell Parish*

Just hear those Al Gore Followers
Quick to swallow his line
Come on it's just the weather
Not a climate catastrophe sign.

Don't need those carbon offsets
Or sign the Kyoto Pact line
Come on it's just the weather
Not a climate catastrophe sign.

We agree, we can see, going green's not bad
Just keep it in hand
No need to worry 'bout our natural land.

Don't despair, we all care, keeping clean our share
Just don't believe all that Al calls for
He's living in fairyland.

Our land is quite remarkable
That Big Blue Marble's so fine
Come on it's just the weather
Not a climate catastrophe sign

It's So Easy Bein' Green
This is for baseballdoc, by request. I can almost hear Kermit singing.
From the original ""It's Not Easy Bein' Green" lyrics by Joe Rapposo

It's So Easy Bein' Green
Just to take Al Gore on trust when he speaks
There's no need to use your ears or eyes, or think, or read
Or something much more difficult like that.

It's So Easy Bein' Green
Just take a stand against so many ordinary things
Like using oil, or drilling for more, or having light
bulbs that are pear-shaped instead of curly -
Or other awful things like that.

But carbon footprints aren't a scam!
Even though Gore's company has more
If we're just 'green' we'll save the oceans, the
atmosphere and animals, or even just a tree.

When green is what it's cool to be
It could make you wonder why, but why wonder? Why Wonder?
If Al Gore says it is true, it's beautiful!
He's done the thinking all for me.

Al Gore
Stem: "Daniel," Music by Elton John, Lyrics by Bernie Taupin

Al Gore is traveling tonight on a plane
I can see his carbon footprints,
Oh but the man is insane
Oh and
I can see Al Gore waving goodbye
God it looks like Al Gore,
With Oscar and the Nobel Prize

He says Earth is dying
And I want to scream
Al says it's in the worst shape
That he's ever seen
Oh and
How could he know?
He's just a big dunce!
Lord I hate Al Gore
And some voted for him once

Al Gore you wacko,
What will your programs cost?
Do you still feel the pain?
From elections you lost?
You might have tried,
But your ambitions died
Al Gore you've got stars
Standing there by your side (repeat)

Al Gore is traveling tonight on a plane
Leaving more carbon footprints,
Oh but the man is insane.
Oh and...
I can see Al Gore wearing a crown
God it looks like no one
Understands he is a clown

God it looks like no one
Understands he is a clown

Uncle Albert
Paul McCarney's song, "Admiral Halsey." For Al Gore! (Of course)

We're so sorry Uncle Albert
We're so sorry if we caused Earth any pain
You're so silly Uncle Albert
In your brain there's no one home
And we believe in sun and rain

We're so sorry that our carbon footprint's on the rise
We're so sorry, Uncle Albert
But we know that in your mind you deserve the Nobel Prize

We're so sorry, Uncle Albert
But we haven't hugged a bloody tree all day
We're so sorry Uncle Albert
But we know your thinking globally will
Carry you away.

Chorus: Land soon under water (water)
Storms across the sky
Polar Bears in danger (danger)
Whose fault? You or I?

Mr. Al Gore he tells us his lies
He says we must conserve or we will not survive
He says the world is sick, with a temperature high, we all will die!

(The glaciers will melt so we all are gonna die)

Land soon under water (water)
Storms across the sky
Polar Bears in danger (danger)
Whose fault? You or I?

Al Gore is a little wacko, so profound (such a clown)
Get our footprints off the ground

Save the planet, bears will drown

Al Gore has a Nobel and an Oscar found (He'll expound)
Get our footprints off the ground
Save the planet, bears will drown

(*Chorus*) Oooo Ooo (*repeat and fade*)

It's Doo-Doo
"Something Stupid" by Robbie Williams.
The following was inspired by the Nick Nichols article of March
1, 2008. Picture an environmental 'wacko' singing this.

You think it is a line
Although I think it is sublime
To add my voice with Al Gore
And when I wander off the ranch
I know that there's a chance
You'll say "Why don't you just hit the door"

'Cause when I say
I must blame you for global warming's rise
Because of CO_2,
Well, then you go and spoil it all
By saying something lucid
Like "It's Doo-Doo."

I can see it in your eyes
That you despise
The same old lies
You've heard from Gore before

And though it's just a lie to you
For me it's true
I've never felt so right before!

You'll practice every day
And find some clever lines to say
To illustrate that Warming's not true
But I tell you to wait
Because we've left it all too late
And don't' you know that we're doomed?

The time is right
Your logic fills my head

The Right is red and
Oh the Left's so blue
And then you go and spoil it all
By saying something lucid
Like "It's doo-doo"

It's doo-doo.
(*Repeat and fade*)

Swallow the Next Episode
Follow the Yellow Brick Road, from the Wizard of Oz, E H Harburg and Music by Harold Arlen

Swallow the next episode, Swallow the next episode
Swallow, Swallow, Swallow, Swallow,
Swallow the next episode.
Although it's politics, Don't be a heretic
Sign on to save our abode!

The world is in a crisis,
The eco-alarms are abuzz
You'll find it is a joke of a hoax,
If ever a hoax there was.
If ever oh ever a hoax there was,
The one Al Gore tells is one because
Because, because, because, because, because.
Because it's junk science that backs it up!
The hoax is global warming!
And what we exhale is the cause.

Al Gore has many faithful,
They swallow his line everyday
Although he tells a whale of a tale,
No logic tears them away.
If ever oh ever a hoax there was,
The one Al Gore tells is one because
Because.....
Because of the penance we have to pay.
To hell with Global Warming,
I really think Earth is Okay!

Polar Bears are Yummy
Another remix of the MASH theme by Altman & Mandel. This was in response to an article on 19 January, 2008, asking if polar bears were edible?

Did you hear about the ice?
They say that Polar Bears are nice
But they are doomed to die you see
And all the blame's on you and me!
But..
Polar bears are yummy
They taste good in my tummy
And I would surely eat one if I could....

I'm sick that bears our species trump
I'd like to kick the Greenie's rumps
The earth did fine without our aid
Send all those bears to the Everglades!
For
Polar bears are Tasty
Although their coats are pasty
And we could surely eat them if we pleased....

Greenies Tap Corn

No Food for Oil is my new mantra. It is our own version of the Oil for Food Scandal. I remember the 70s and I see the folly in the politicians stating 'we can't drill our way out' of this mess, etc. etc. Why can't we both drill and build refineries for the short term, and explore other ways to achieve energy independence in the meantime? Why does it have to be either/or?

From Blue Tail Fly (Jimmy Crack Corn)

When I was young I used to wait
To fill my car and it warn't great
Cause Jimmy Carter got it all wrong
And now we're dancing to a similar song

Greenies Tap Corn, and they don't care
Greenies Tap Corn, and they don't care
Greenies Tap Corn, and they don't care
That Food has gone away.

Now with ethanol as our gas
I see we will repeat the past
Instead of a drill to increase supply
The Congress chose to spit in our eye

(*Chorus*)

Some day our Congress will replay
The policies they enact today
When food is scarce and oil is high
The devil take those blue-tail guys

(*Chorus*)

Why can't they see we must be bold?
We should be pumping ANWR gold
No more the Middle East to tap

And no more corn to fill in the gap!

(*Chorus*)

Now is the time our pols to warn
We need oil but not from corn
Nuclear energy is a boon
We're victims of that Al Gore loon
(*Chorus, repeat and fade*)

Why Not Drill?

This is the longest parody I have written. It is from Rodgers & Hammerstein's 'Carousel' and is called "Soliloquy" but is most often thought of as "My Boy Bill." I expect that unless you are a die-hard musical fan you may not recognize this song! I hope you make it to the end!

I wonder when he'll get a clue?
I guess we'll call him the 'old man'
We can compare Maverick To the other feller's blather
'Yes, we can.'
I bet that he'll turn out to be
The spittin' image of a Lib
But he's got more common sense
Than his puddin'-head opponent ever did!
Can we teach him to wrestle
Our borders to save
When he's off to the White House as our chief?
We all wish he'd take on
A way to be brave
But he's always a missin' our relief!
That's him! That's McCain! No Drills!

Drill.....
If we'd drill
Our fair nation will see a new day, we will!
Why not drill? And with all
We can still save a tree! Just drill!
If we just drill now
With our head held high
And we capture that oil from the ground
You won't see nobody dare to try
To boss us or toss us around!
No Saudi Arabian bullies
Will toss us around!

I don't give a hang what he's done

As long as he'll do what is right!
He sat on his tail
In a prisoner's jail
While Barry wasn't even in sight!
If he'll just change his tune on the border
Stop being a partisan hack
Stop crossing the aisle
Making Liberals Smile
Take the knife from Conservatives' back!

Our great nation dug the Erie Canal
Put a man named Armstrong on the moon!
A President asked, the Berlin Wall crashed
Of course it takes talent to sing that tune!

Aha-ha-ha-ha!
He could be the champ of Conservatives!
What's a feller like me to do?
For the President of the United States
I'd like a man who's true!

But he won't be President
Not if he don't get a clue!
Just Drill!!!!

If we'd drill
Our fair nation will see a new day, we will!
If we just drill now with our heads held high
And we capture that oil from the ground
You won't see nobody dare to try
To boss us or toss us around
No Saudi Arabian, Terrorist state-ian, OPEC co-nation, Bullies!
Will toss us around!

And I'm hanged if I'll vote for the B. Obama
A Dumbo-eared liberal that oozes drama
Who'll hang with OPEC

And pull out our troops
And turn our allies to rejection....
Hey! What are we? American dupes?
We ain't even had the election!!

So what if John McCain is seventy or so?
Isn't that the new Fifty-five?
He's had more experience, has more to show
Than before Obama was alive!
I can tell you....
Wait a minute...
Could it be?
What the hell!
What if he refuses to drill?
What could we do then?
What will we do for fuel?
No Fun! No Money!
We could have fun with the sun
But you've got to take it farther now and drill!
It mightn't be so bad to do
A little respite from despair
We could be cool with more fuel
While we worked on other measures
What a pair!!!

Drilling for oil
Not so bad, nor will we despoil the land!
Drilling for oil
Is just the sweetest gift
While we improve our plan
Why should we take a back seat?
While other nations thrive?
Do what they can to get heat!
We, too, must survive!

We have a few Green and Clean young people,
No earth to spoil

But drilling for oil
Will never cause the blight of living without oil!

We've got to get ready before 'Want' comes
We've got to make certain that he
Won't be swayed by the thought
That our oil is naught, by Greens!

We've got a great nation
We must survive
Lest our way of life not thrive!
We surely know how to make money!
So let's try, let's try! Let's Try!
Don't let China kill it! We will it!
Let's Drill it!!!!! Or DIE!

Drillin' Drillin' Drillin'
By request, for my friend, Farmer's Wife. To the tune of the Rawhide Theme (again!)

Keep drillin', drillin', drilllin'
Our gas tanks need fillin'
Pump some oil we're willin'
McHyde!
Don't try to please those greenies!
Who cares if we are meanies!
Just use your conscience as your guide!
There's lots of oil in ANWR,
It's better than some coal-tar
And I don't want to give up my ride!

Take a stand, Get a pump
Add some life to your stump
Get some oil, From our soil, McHyde!
Don't go left, show some class
Take a stand, kick some ass
Get some oil, from our soil, McHYDE!

Drillin' drillin' drillin'
Don't you know we're willin'?
Stop that Kool-aid swillin'
McHyde!
Solar and Wind together
Won't this shortage weather
Why won't you take our nation's side?
Soon we'll all be missin'
Good vittles, won't you listen?
Start drilling for our own oil supplies!

Take a stand, pump it up
Add some life to your stump
Get some oil, From our soil, McHyde!
Stop your guff, show some class

Take a stand, kick some ass
Get some oil, from our soil, McHYDE!

McHyde! [Whip crack!]
McHyde! [Whip crack!]

Get you Some Victimhood
From Sam the Sham and the Pharohs' 'Little Red Riding Hood' by Ronald Blackwell

Owoooooo!
Who's that we see talkin' victimhood?
Why Didn't you think that Barry would?
Hey there get you some victimhood
Those prospects look real good
You're everything a big bad liberal could want
Listen to me!
Listen to Hollywood
They all think that Jimmy Carter's good!
He's walking to see Mahmoud and Hamas alone
Owooooo!
What big ears you have
The kind of ears that Dumbo has
Why don't you tune in; not cop out
If you won't listen maybe then we'll shout.
What loose lips you have
You hang around with some who're bad
So before you place more Blago's shame
I think you ought to embrace your middle name.

Some bitter folks have guns to tote
We will need them for our vote
'Cause we don't trust you'll leave our second Amendment alone.
Owooooo!
Grab you some victimhood
Like Wright and Ayers say you should
But we might think they aren't so great so we won't!
Owooooo!

What a big heart you have-
The better to sell your plan
Barry Obama-man,
Black or White?

To me you're Tan.
Go on and see naught but race,
Slander us to our face
Maybe you have won the race
But we expect White House disgrace
Hey there Grab you some Victimhood
Hope sure is sounding good
You're everything that a big bad liberal could want
Owoooooo!
I mean Bah!!!!
Baaaaah!

Ebony and Ivory
Ebony and Ivory" by Paul McCartney. Since Obama is bi-racial, this song seems to call out for a parody. I wish the media and candidate placed more emphasis on qualifications and less on race. Curious that he identifies with his Blackness when he is equally White.

Ebony and Ivory
Live together in Barack's family tree
Black or White?
He could be either one, son,
Oh but,
Which is he?

We all know
That liberals look at race where ever we go
There is good and bad
In every face
But it is race,
It's race that gives Obama
What he needs to excel
He's learned it so well.

Ebony and Ivory
Live together in Barack's family tree
Black or White?
He could be either one, son,
Oh but,
Which is he?
(Repeat and fade)

Bad Race Relations
The Beach Boys' "Good Vibrations"

I....I see the colorful clothes he wears
And the way that Jeremiah jumps and swears
I would like the sound of a gentle word
Or the proof that makes me think Obama cares

I'm picking up bad vibrations
They're talking down my great nation
(Oom bop bop bad vibrations)
I'm listening to accusations
(oom bop bop accusations)
Bad, Bad, Bad, Race Relations
(Oom bop bop)
He's spouting more defamation
(oom bop bop defamation)
Bad, Bad, Bad race relations
(oom bop bop)
He's handing us obfuscation
(Oom bop bop obfuscation)

Close your eyes
Don't watch Obama now
Listen close, You know you must be 'blind '
Look closer into his eyes
And you know he shares those racist ties

I'm picking up bad vibrations
The race card's in escalation
I'm picking up bad vibrations
(oom bop bop bad vibrations)
The race card's in escalation
(oom bop bop escalation)
Bad, bad, bad race relations
(oom bop bop)
He's handing us explanations
(oom bop bop explanations)

Bad, bad, bad race relations
(oom bop bop)
But it's just equivocation!
(oom bop bop equivocation)

AAAHHHHHH!

(Ah my my observation)
I don't know where but he should go there
(he is an abomination)
(Ah Christian impersonation)
(Ah my my What?)

Gotta keep my eye on Obama
He is panderin' to us
Gotta seek the truth when
Obama is selling us 'no fuss'
Gotta hear those Obamanations are happening

AAAHHHHHH!

Bad, bad, bad race relations
(oom bop bop)
(I'm hearing more 'damn the nation')
He's saying there's justification
(oom bop bop)
(Obfuscation)
Bad, bad, bad race relations
(Oom bop bop)
Just say Nah!....
Na na na na na
Na na na
Na na na na na
Na na na
No no no no no
No no no
No no no no no
No no no....

Obama Played the Race Card
Peter, Paul and Mary's folk song, "Stewball"

Obama played the race card,
And he thinks that's just fine
He never drank kool-aid,
Just sells the party line

His tongue it is silver,
His opponent is old
And the worth of his prattle
Will never be gold

Oh the fairgrounds were crowded,
Obama was there
And the betting was heavy,
That he'd beat Clinton's share.

And a-way up yonder,
Ahead what at sight,
Came a-prancin' and a-dancin'
That old Reverend Wright.

I bet on the Clintons ,
I bet on McCain
If I'd a bet on Obama,
I'd be a free man again.

Oh the race card is hollow,
Don't you think he should-a known?
Now Obama's in trouble,
And he's got to go home.

Obama played the race card,
And he thought that was fine.
I bet he regrets now,
That he drank Wright's whine.

The Reverend Jeremiah Wright
*The Reverend Mr. Black (Johnny Cash) written
by Billy Edd Wheeler and Jed Peters*

[*Spoken*]
He spoke loudly in Chicago he was black and mean
And at first you'd a thought no one could be that obscene
But one look in his church and an ear to his song
Showed a man like Wright to be outright wrong.
He was a racist preacher man, and I want you to know
He could preach such hate he could melt the snow.
He married Obama and Michelle, in fact,
And folks all knew his church was just for blacks.
He came off as a hater, not a bit like King
And sometimes in the evening I could hear him sing:

(*Chorus*)

You gotta walk that hate-filled valley
You gotta walk it with my help
Oh nobody White can walk it for you
You got to walk it with my help.

[*Spoken*]

If ever I thought to join Obama's camp
Thought his 'hope' and 'audacity' made him a champ
I gave that notion up the day
I heard the things his preacher had to say.
It wasn't enough that his wife was not proud
When she criticized our nation before a crowd.
But when he thought he was leading the race
Obama spoke up: insulted us to our face!
He showed himself to be a typical mule
And to my way of thinkin' it took a real fool,
To say that we were bitter and gun-totin' hacks
Bat that's what he said, and he cannot take it back!

He'll sink like a rock, that man among men
And we won't tolerate all those insults again
And now with a voice as strong as can be
We'll cut him down like a big old tree when we sing:

(*Chorus*)

You gotta stop that campaign Barry
You gotta stop it by yourself
For anybody else is better than you
Put your campaign upon the shelf.

[*Spoken*]

It's been many years since King and Rosa Parks
And I really think our nation took their cause to heart
I can still hear those inspirational echoes ring
When he emphasized our character, that Reverend Dr. King
We followed him, yes sir, and we can't regret it
And I only wish Barry would be a credit
To his memory! 'Cause I want you to understand
The U.S.A. is still a great, great land!

(*Chorus*)

We gotta get a better leader
We gotta raise up a campaign
That we'll gladly follow with conviction
And U.S.A. will shine again!

For Twenty Years He Listened
Theme from MASH "Suicide is Painless"
Mike Altman & Johnny Mandel

Did you hear what he said today?
B.O. is going to walk away
To Trinity he says farewell
He's not a part of what they sell.

For Twenty Years he listened
But Scrutiny's spotlight glistened
And now his resignation's on the way.

And though he says it makes him sad
He must think all of us are mad
Can we forget they played a part
In molding B. Obama's heart?

For Twenty Years he listened
Til Scrutiny's spotlight glistened
And resignations don't take that away

With those big ears I think he must
Have got the gist, believed the thrust
Of what those Reverends had to say
And only now he walks away?

For Twenty Years he listened
Til Scrutiny's spotlight glistened
And resignations won't wash that away

How stupid does he think we are?
Does he intend to raise the bar?
Or can he only bob and weave
Which? He or Trinity believe?

For Twenty Years he listened
Til Scrutiny's spotlight glistened
And distance doesn't make that disappear.

It almost seems as if he must
Protect his church from scrutiny's thrust
He wants that spotlight all on him
That O' Messiah bit's grown dim

For B. Obama's running
And I think he is cunning
He knows the voters will forget and cheer
I guess we'll find out in another year.

Get Back Honky
Elton John's "Honky Cat"

When we look back,
Boy, he must have been green
Hopping cross the country
And the voters scream
Looking for an answer, tryin for color-blind
Until we saw your Reverend Wright
Honey we was blind

He said get back honky cat
Better get back from our hood
You should quit your clinging to those redneck things
And oh,mmmmmmmm oh the Change is gonna do you good.

They said Get Back Honky Cat
Voting for Obama is where it's at
You're just trying to find truth in a guilty mind
It's like, not so very risky, Oh buy into my whine.

Well I read some books and I saw some magazines
About that big debacle down in New Orleans
And all the Democrats, well, said I was a tool
They said, Don't you think that Bush is just a bigger fool?

Get back honky cat
Better get back from our hood
You should quit your clinging to those redneck things
And oh,mmmmmmmm oh the Change is gonna do you good.

(*Piano riff*)

Get back honky cat
Better get back from our hood
You should quit your clinging to those redneck things
And oh,mmmmmmmm oh the Change is gonna do you good.

They said go back home
Boy, Our campaign's full of charm
Living History ain't enough, Old Hill has bought the farm
But how can we stay, when our heart says no
How can we vote when he's just B.O.?

Get back honky cat
Better get back from our hood
You should quit your clinging to those redneck things
And oh,mmmmmmmm oh the Change is gonna do you good.

You'd better Get Back Honky Cat
Voting for Obama is where it's at
You're just trying to find truth in a guilty mind
It's like, not so very risky, oh just buy into my whine.

Get Back Honky Cat, Get Back Honky
Cat, Get Back OOOOH (*repeat*)

Let's Talk Some More 'bout Race
'Put on a Happy Face' from 'Bye, Bye Birdie' (Adams & Strouse)

Hey guys I'm gonna gear up
Just hear my view on race
Wise guys may want to clear up
Doubts about Barry's grace
I think you're all self-segregationists
But in a while
You'll see that we can keep you on a list
Watch your profile!

I've got a diff'rent playbook
AG with racial spin
Look for the newest white book
Big Brother watches sin
But soon: Breadlines all over the place!
So, let's talk some more 'bout race!

(musical interlude)

Let's talk some more 'bout race!
Let's talk some more 'bout race!
D' Da Da Da D' Da Da Da

Hey Guys We're gonna Change You
It's just like white on rice
Weekends we'll rearrange too
You need to treat us nice
And if you're feeling 'cross' and bitterish
We'll sit and whine
Think of vanilla cream and licorice
And we'll feel fine!

I know you're feeling gloomy
But we're in charge: We Won
Now you just listen to me
Racism is our gun
And we'll push it right into your face
Let's talk some more 'bout race!
So, let's talk some more 'bout race!

Chapter Three:
Politicians

Jimmy Carter

That Ding A Ling

Former President Jimmy Carter went on yet another 'peace' trip to rub elbows with Hamas and others like his old friend, Arafat. To call him a Ding A Ling is the nicest thing I can say about his shameful behavior. 'My Ding A Ling' original by Chuck Barry

When Jimmy was a little bitty boy
He thought he'd be to earth a joy
Truth is he don't know a thing
But we all know he's a ding a ling

That Ding a Ling, that Ding a Ling
I wish he'd stop negotiating
That Ding a Ling, That Ding a Ling
I think he believes he's America's King

And when Jimmah props up that Arafat tool
We all should see that he is a fool
Every time he takes to wing
We all can see he's a Ding a Ling

Once he was honored with that old Peace Prize
What can you say about that? 'Surprise!'
If we could think it meant a thing
We might be proud of the Ding a Ling

Now old Jimmah is greeting Hamas
He lends his aid like he was the boss
Lays a wreath at Arafat's tomb
That Ding a Ling needs a padded room!

Some say Jimmy has a right
To travel and prop up the terrorist might
To those who think he is beyond the pale
Pick up his passport and throw him in jail

That Ding a ling, That Ding a Ling
I think he believes he's Humanity's King
That Ding a ling, That Ding a Ling
Wake up, America, Ding a ling a ling!

Jimmy Rat!
*Another parody to Jimmy Carter. I hate that he is
negotiating with terrorists. Revoke his passport!
This one is from the Vandella's "Jimmy Mack"*

Jimmy Rat, Jimmy, oh Jimmy Rat, why don't you go right back?
Jimmy Rat, Jimmy, oh Jimmy Rat, why don't you go right back?

Hamas is missing you,
Iran feels the same way too
You've tried so hard you big fool,
Like you promised you'd do
But this boy keeps trav'ling around,
He's trying to wear a peacemakers crown

Hey Jimmy, Jimmy, oh Jimmy Rat, why don't you go right back?
Hey Jimmy, Jimmy, oh Jimmy Rat, why don't you go right back?

He wanders all alone,
Talking peace, but we're at war!
He's a fool, to Terrorists blind,
Just like he was before
And this 'Chamberlain' with the big grin
Keeps reaching out to be their friend.

(*Chorus*)
No more passport, no more passport
[instrumental break]

I wanna say,
We don't want you any longer,
We need to make the Logan act stronger
You go to see Mahmoud,
But Jimmy, he talks just the same as you

(*Chorus*)

No more passport, no more passport
(*repeat*)
Jimmy, Jimmy, oh Jimmy Rat, we all don't want you back

Welcome Back Cah-tah!
Theme song from Welcome Back Kotter
original by John Sebastian

Welcome Back,
You're dreaming, but check it out

Welcome Back,
To that hope and change that Barry lied about

Well some names are the same as the Carter years
Add some more Clintonistas, he'll keep them near

Who'd have thought he'd lead ya
(Who'd have thought he'd lead ya)
Back there while he knee'd ya
(Don't swear! But he knee'd ya!)

Yeah we hit the jackpot and can't do diddley-squat,
welcome back
welcome back,
welcome back,
welcome back

John Edwards

Don't Have a Neutron's Chance

Another friend from Townhall inspired the following parody of then-candidate, John Edwards, when she wrote "I don't think Edwards is as deep as paper. A piece of paper has substance, and is useful. He lacks both qualities. He has the depth of a neutron, and just as effective." So this one was written for you, YLG!

'Neutron Dance' by the Pointer Sisters

I'm John Edwards, I'm your candidate
Don't you think my hairstyle is first-rate?
Ambulances used to be my beat
Now the other candidates will see defeat

Whoo oooh
Whoo oooh

Don't you like to hear my southern drawl?
I've got more to say than that old man, Ron Paul
No one else can match my intellect
All the rest are bad, I know how to collect

Whoo ooh
Whoo ooh

(*Chorus*)
Even though you say
You don't believe a word I say
And my wife you'll see
Who's the one to speak for me
I'm just learning,
Don't have a neutron's chance
I'm just learning,
Don't have a neutron's chance

Candidates will lie and that's for sure

Don't believe me when I say I love the poor
Proof is there if you will only look
'Cause everything I say is gobbledegook

(*Chorus*)

Whoo oooh
Whoo oooh
I'm a loser, yeah
I'm a loser, yeah

(*Chorus*)

I doubt there's a pot of gold for me
No matter how I try to just believe
And I'm just learning,
Don't have a neutron's chance
I'm just learning,
Don't have a neutron's chance
Campaign's burning,
Don't have a neutron's chance.

**Remix of Don't have a Neutron's Chance
[following his 'indescretion']**

I'm John Edwards, Was a candidate
Don't you think my hairstyle is first-rate?
Ambulances used to be my beat
Now the paparazzi's puttin' on the heat!

Whoo oooh
Whoo oooh

Don't you like to hear my southern drawl?
Reporters heard me in that bathroom stall
No one else can match my stealthy act
A love child's on my head and I cannot take it back

Whoo oooh
Whoo oooh

(*Chorus*)
Even though you say
You don't believe a word I say
It's my wife you'll see
Who's the one I cheated, see?
I'm just learning, don't have a neutron's chance
I'm just learning, don't have a neutron's chance

Candidates will lie and that's for sure
Don't believe me when I say I love the poor
Proof is there if you will only look
'Cause everything I say is gobbledegook

(*Chorus*)
Even though you say
You don't believe a word I say
It's my wife you'll see
That's been cheated more by me

I'm just learning, don't have a neutron's chance
I'm just learning, don't have a neutron's chance

Whoo ooh
Whoo ooh
I'm a loser, yeah
I'm a loser, yeah
(*Chorus*)
Even though you say
You don't believe a word I say
It's my kids you'll see
Who're humiliated, see?
I'm just learning, don't have a neutron's chance
I'm just learning, don't have a neutron's chance

I doubt there is a White House spot for me
No matter how I try to just believe
And I'm just learning, don't have a neutron's chance
I'm just learning, don't have a neutron's chance
Campaign's burning, don't have a neutron's chance

Caught You Mr. Ed

It was inevitable! Someone referred to John Edwards as Mr. Ed. So here it is! From the TV sitcom Mr. Ed. (Mr Ed Original Theme by Ray Evans and Jay Livingston)

Divorce is a course to force, of course
And no one can talk to the source, of course
That is, of course, unless divorce is the
Fate of Mr. Ed.

Go right to the source and ask, of course
He'll give you the answer he must endorse
He never thinks the truth has force
Lies from Mr. Ed.

People magazine soon will speak,
And spread more Breck Girl lies
But Mr. Ed will only streak
Pretending he's found a disguise!

Divorce is a course to force, of course
And it's not the usual 'suit' he sports
A baby's here from intercourse?

Well listen to this.
Caught you, Mr. Ed!

Mike Huckabee

Huckabee Do Dah!

*In January, Mike Huckabee had a surprise victory
in the Iowa caucus (so did Obama).
From Song of the South.
The Oscar-winning song: Zipadee Doo Dah!
By Ray Gilbert & Allie Wrubel*

Huckabee Do Dah, Huckabee ay
He just won the race in Old Eye Oh Way
Plenty of voters, headin' his way
Huckabee Do Dah, Huckabee's day

Will he keep momentum rolling?
Or will he, like we've seen
Be another flash like old Dean?
Huckabee Do Dah, Huckabee's day
We all are reeling, reeling today!

Huckabee Do Dah, Huckabee ay
Why oh why is Hunter treated this way?
He came in third in Wyoming you say?
Duncan is better, better I say!

Old Fred Thompson and Mitt Romney
There's McCain and Rudy
Each debate's like Punch and Judy
Huckabee Do Dah, Huckabee Ay
Who will deliver? Who is to say?

Obama trampled, Hillary's day
My, oh, my, why isn't that great you say?
But now Obama's headin' our way
Who will deliver, who is to say?

If we get another RINO
He won't win, that's factual
Just Conservatives have got pull
Huckabee Do Dah, Huckabee's Day
We all are reeling, reeling today!

Elliot Spitzer

New York New York

The Elliot Spitzer prostitution scandal began on March 10, 2008, when The New York Times reported that Democratic New York Governor Elliot Spitzer had patronized a prostitution service called Emperors Club VIP. The prostitute was called 'Kristen" and Spitzer was identified as 'client-9." The scandal ultimately led him to announce his resignation as governor on March 12, effective March 17, 2008. New York, New York (Frank Sinatra) by Ebb and Kander

I'm there in the news, I'm leaving today
They say they want no part of me, New York, New York
That prostitute's list, Well, what can I say?
That client number nine is me, New York, New York

I used to be a crusader (a quantum leap!)
But now I'm there in the muck, not top of the heap

Those demo-state 'Blues,' are melting away
To scrutiny thought I was immune-in old New York
If I can't make it there, we all are doomed, I swear
Could not fool you, New York, New York

New York, New York
I used to wake up next to Kristen while my wife sleeps
And find I'm just number nine - down on the list
Who woulda thought
What a cruel twist!

Those Wall Street folks yell, they're happy today
They're glad to see me down and out, in old New York
And.....
This guy who used to be an Emperor's VIP
Has got to leave New York, New York!

Ron Blagojevich

Who Are the People with Blagojevich?
From Sesame Street: Who Are the People in Your Neighborhood?
*[pronounced: Blah **goy**' a vitch]*

Who are the people with Blagojevich?
Don't ya think it's rich?
Ain't life just a bitch?
Oh who are the People with Blagojevich?
Watch and see who's in the buses' way.

Why did Obama flee the neighborhood?
Says he's just a hood
Up to no darn good
And why did Obama flee the Neighborhood
Was Blagojevich just in his way?

Oh now who will nominate his Senate seat
Get his Senate seat?
Will they lie and cheat?
Get ready to listen to old Durbin preach
Now that Governor Blago is out

When will we fully see Chicago thugs
Picture all their mugs
Will they still be smug?
And how long can Barry give it all a shrug?

They're the people that he needs,
With those ACORNs planting seeds
Now they're people that he'll toss away

Hillary Rodham Clinton

Fearful, Queasy Feeling
"Peaceful, Easy Feeling" by the Eagles

I hate the way Hil'ry Clinton says
She has a plan to take our dough
And she's gonna keep the oil profits from those
Who already earned it, ya know?
'Cause I get a fearful, queasy feeling
And I know she'll just let us down
'Cause she's already claiming
She owns the crown.

I found out a long time ago
What a Clinton can do to your soul
Ah, but a vote for Hill is a vote for Bill
Or visa versa, don't ya know?
'Cause I get a fearful, queasy feeling
And I know she'll just let us down
'Cause she's already claiming
She owns the crown.

I get a feeling no one knows her well
As a Senator or a friend
But her voice keeps screeching
In my other ear, and tells me
We may ne'er see America again
'Cause I get a fearful, queasy feeling
And I know she'll just let us down
'Cause she's already claiming she owns the crown.

'Cause she's already claiming she owns the crown...
Ooooooo , ooooooooo

I hate the way that Hil'ry Clinton says
she has a plan to take our dough

and she's gonna keep the oil
profits from those
who already earned it ya know?
'cause I get a fearful, queasy feeilng
and I know she'll let us down
'cause she's already claiming
To own the crown
I found out a long time ago
What a Clinton can do to your soul
Ah, but a vote for Hill is a vote for Bill
Or Visa versa, don't ya know?
'cause I get a fearful, queasy feeling,
And I know she'll let us down
'cause she's already claiming she owns the crown

I get a feeling no one knows her
as a Senator or friend
But this voice keeps whispering
in my other ear, tells me
We may never see America again
'cause I get a fearful, queasy feeling,
And I know she'll let us down
'cause she's already claiming
She owns the crown
'cause she's already claiming
She owns the crown...oooo, oooo

She'll Spin it Easy
From Ringo Starr's 'It Don't Come Easy"

She'll spin it easy, you know she'll spin it easy
She'll spin it easy, you know she'll spin it easy

Do what Hilly says or she might not be the Prez
She can win the prize quite easy
Don't fret 'bout what to do, she can silence Mr. Hsu
It's enough to make you queasy

Don't look into her past, no trouble borrow
From first lady to the Prez, Brave New World is our tomorrow

She don't ask for much, she just wants us to trust
She can fix health care quite easy
Don't worry about Bill, he's just a useful shill
He'll fit in the White House easy

Don't worry that he'll add a little drama
He understands the game and will help her beat Obama

Forget about the facts, she'll only raise your tax
Funding socialism's easy
She knows what she wants to do, it don't matter about you
She will pick our pockets easy

Imagine Hillary and another hurricane
FEMA will be strong because Bush no longer is to blame

She needs soft balls at debates for Clinton to relate
She will say her planning's centrist
She'll get her votes from you, and all illegals too
She'll exact her plan with interest

Worried that we get a dual president?
She'll just say, "Not true, Bill is just a legal resident."

Do what Hilly says or she might not be the Prez
She has MSM to tell you
She wants a social state, not revisit travelgate
It's enough to make you queasy.

She'll spin it easy, she says she'll win it easy...
We all feel queasy, you know we all feel queasy....

Do It My Way

There is a certain irony to writing a parody about the author of It Takes a Village by using the Village People's mega-hit **Y-M-C-A**.

Hey there, there's no need to feel down
Hey there people,
Hillary is in town
Hey there People, I am nobody's clown
I am sure to solve your problems

Village, that's my claim to success
I say, village,
Forget your happiness
I say, village, just give up your largess
Many ways to share your money

I'm always saying just Do It My Way
I'm always saying just Do It My Way
I have everything in my able control
Clintonomics is on a roll?

I'm always saying just Do It My Way
I'm always saying just Do It My Way
You can give me your dough,
You'll have health care for free,
I have plans just listen to me...

Comrade, are you listening to me?
I said, Comrade,
Aren't you sad to be free?
I said, Comrade
I can make real your dreams
But you got to know this one thing!

No man does it all by himself.
I said, Comrade,
Put your dreams on the shelf,

And just listen, trust this woman today
I am sure you'll see it my way...

I'm always saying just Do It My Way
I'm always saying just Do It My Way
I have everything in my able control
Clintonomics is on a roll?

I'm always saying just Do It My Way
I'm always saying just Do It My Way
You can give me your dough,
You'll have health care for free
I have plans just listen to me....

Comrade, I was once in your shoes.
And I Hear You,
And you're singing the blues
But I will help you so just look in my eyes
All the world I will hypnotize

Now then, forget freedom and such
I will fix us
And I won't ask for much
I know best how to handle your woes
Only tell your cash Adios...

I'm always saying just Do It My Way
I'm always saying just Do It My Way
I'm the smartest you see,
Come on listen to me
Just hand over the country to me!

I'm always saying just Do It My Way
I'm always saying just Do It My Way
You can give me your dough,
You'll have health care for free
I have plans just listen to me.

I'm Just a Socialist
From WHAM! "Love Machine"

I'm just a Socialist
And you won't work for nobody but me
I'm just a Socialist
A money grabbin' fiend.
I think it's high time you knew
Whenever I think of you
I see Marx is true.
When I look to the polls
My meter starts to roll, and I become confused.
My centrist demeanor shows
When I'm getting set to run
Elect Mrs. C. Ain't it fun,
And my inflated ego will grow- woooo

I'm just a Socialist
And you won't work for nobody but me
I'm just a Socialist
A money grabbin' fiend.

Na, na na na na, na na na na, woo-woo-wooo
Na, na na na na, na na na na, na naaah
I'm just a Socialist....
[repeat ad nauseum]

I Need Money
Beatles' classic, "Money"

The best thing for U.S. is me
There is no need to vote the G.O.P.
(Chorus)

Now give me money
That's what I want
That's want I want, yeah
That's what I want

I have plans for everything it's true
You know what I decide you can use
(Chorus)

My vote will Socialism bring
Capitalism is so right-wing
(Chorus)

Democrats will all your dreams fulfill
The G.O.P. won't pay your bills
(Chorus)

You're votes give me such a thrill
You're a lot more fun than Bill
(Chorus)

Well now give me money
Vote for me Honey
Wow, yeah, just you vote for me
Power is my fantasy
That's what I want
That's what I want, well
Now give me money
A lot of money
Wow, yeah, I need Money
From Hsu, more money
That's what I want, yeah
That's what I want

I Agonize
Johnny Cash's "I Walk the Line"

I keep a close watch on old Hillary
She tells us all we'll have health care for free
If she's elected danger I foresee
Because she lies, I agonize

I find it very, very easy to be blue
The MSM keeps saying she'll be true
Yes, I'll even say it's true she is a shrew
Because she lies, I agonize

As sure as day is light and night is dark
We saw Vince Foster laying in a park
Do we once more into those days embark?
Because she lies, I agonize.

She has a way to keep us on the dole
Her scandals soon will rival grassy knoll
She's just like Bill and listens to the polls
Because she lies, I agonize.

I keep a close watch on those Liberal scum
I wish they'd all go back from where they come
Soon we'll be singing, 'We Shall Overcome'
Because she lies, I agonize

Be Our Guarantor
Beatles' "When I'm 64"

When we're all stuck with Hillarycare
A few years from now
Will you still be handling your family's health
Choose your doctor, keeping your wealth?
If you will find you need surgery
Will the wait be more?
Will it be better, if we just let her
Be our guarantor?

OOOOOOOO

Bill will be there too
And if we let them in
I think I might spew

Will she be handy, leading a war
When she hates our troops
Will she close down GITMO and just set them free
Let Al Qeada hit you and me?
She'll tell the generals making the plans
Don't you ask for more!
Will we be safer, will she shoot straighter
When she guards the door?

I can still remember when the Clintons had the House of White
And it was a mess!
Bill would tell such lies
Interns were on their knees
And Vince Foster died.

Send her a message, let down your hair
Stating point of view
Indicate precisely that she has to stop
Yours sincerely, No agitprop

Give her your answer, send out your vote
Don't you let her score
It won't be better, if we just let her
Be our guarantor.

I've Been Through the Wringer
"Horse With No Name" Written by Dewey Bunnell

When we first elected Clinton
Bill was looking just like the rest
He was calm and tall just a good old boy
He could talk a good line with the best
The first thing he did was expand women's choice
With more funding and new drugs
When he opened his mouth the hot air rose
And his cronies were found to be thugs

(*Chorus*)
I've been through the wringer with a Clinton in charge
It was hard to be up beat in pain
But at least we all can remember his name
Don't forget his wife will be more of the same
La, la...

After two terms with Billy Clinton in charge
Our country was in a spin
They impeached Bill on the Senate floor
Pretty soon Vince Foster was dead
And with Whitewater, Travelgate all adding there too
Bill would lie and sold Lincoln's bed

(*Chorus*)

After eight years we now have old Hillary
It don't make much sense to me
Why'd we choose to put them back in charge
When we really want to be free?
The POTUS is a person with a hand on the phone
Don't you want someone who's sane?
In the White House, oh please remember their name
Cause the Clintons were there and brought us all shame

(*Chorus*)

You've Got to Change
From Santana's "Evil Ways" by Clarence Henry

You've got to change your evil ways, Hilly
If you want us to vote for you
You've got to change, Hilly
We don't think that what you say is true
You got us cryin' and weepin' all over town
You say Obama and Oprah are running you down
This can't go on, Lord knows you got to change, Hilly.

When you come 'round, Hilly,
Your words are harsh and your voice is cold
You send out old Billy,
But even with him you might implode
We're getting tired of hearing of scandals again
We need somebody who don't need to be in the pen
You can't go on, Lord knows you got to change, Hilly.

You can't go home, Hilly
White House is there for the people's choice
We don't want more Billy
You both are bad as our country's voice
We don't want health care, or taxes, or more Bill foolin' 'round
We want somebody who won't make us look like a clown
This can't go on, Lord knows you got to change Hilly

She's A Loser
"I'm a Loser" by (Lennon/McCartney)

She's a loser
She's a loser
And she's not what she appears to be

Of all elections we've won or have lost
There is one name no one ever should cross
She has support of Hsu's millions, my friend
We should have known she might win in the end

She's a loser
And she hasn't got integrity
She's a loser
And she's not what she appears to be

Although she laughs and pretends she's no clown
Beneath that mask she is wearing a frown
Our tears will soon fall like rain from the sky
Is it for her or ourselves that we cry?

She's a loser
And she hasn't got integrity
She's a loser
Cause she's not what she appears to be

(*Harmonica solo, guitar riff*)

What have we done to deserve such a fate?
I really fear that we've left it to late
And it is true, the election's this fall
Don't vote for her or we might lose it all

She's a loser
And she hasn't got integrity
She's a loser
And she's not what she appears to be

She Says She is for Changin'
All the Democrats had the same message: Change
'The Times They Are A-Changin' - Billy Joel.

Come gather 'round people where e'er you call home
And you'll see that the voters around you have shown
That no matter if Clinton's campaign will be blown
If the state to you is worth savin'
Then you'd best cast your vote so she'll sink like a stone
For she says she is for changin'

Come voters and critics who will compare her to men
Just keep your eyes wide
The chance won't come again
And MSM sells you their own brand of spin
And there's no tellin' who that it's namin'
For the loser now might be later to win
For she says she is for changin'

Come Senators, Congressmen, please heed our call
Don't do things all your way
We'll make you all crawl
For he that's elect will be he who has balls
There's a battle outside and it's ragin'
It is here on our borders and we want the wall
For the times they are a-changin'

Come mothers and fathers throughout the land
We must criticize what some don't understand
Our sons and our daughters inherit this land
Our country we must engage in
Let us defeat Clinton we don't need her command
For she says she is for changin'

The time it is here your vote you must cast
Uphold our state let our liberty last
Don't let our freedoms fall into the past
Our nation is rapidly fadin'
Stop her before the blue dye is cast
For she says she is for changin'

I'll Cry if I Want To
Lesley Gore's hit song, "It's My Party" upon the occasion of Hillary's tears during the campaign.

It's my Party and I'll cry if I want to
Cry if I need to, cry to make you Blue
You would cry to if it happened to you

Nobody knows why Obama has surged
But Iowa votes made him win
Why weren't they voting for me?
A her is much better than him

It's my time now, and I'll cry if I want to
Cry if I need to, cry until you spew
Bill would cry too if it made you vote blue

Now all the pundits were talking all night
But they underestimate me
Not til I win the House White
Will I be ready to flee

It's my time now, and I'll cry if I want to
Cry if I need to, cry until you spew
Bill would cry too if it made you vote blue

Just watch my campaign it has only begun
I'm like a Queen with her King
Wait for th' election surprise
When I will win the whole thing

It's my time now, and I'll cry if I want to
Cry if I need to, cry until you spew
Bill will cry too if it makes you vote blue

Oh Oh Oh
It's my time now and I'll cry if I want to
Cry if I need to...Cry until you spew
(repeat and fade)

Boo Hoo Hoo
"Say, Say, Say," -words and music by Paul
McCartney and Michael Jackson.
As sung by Hillary.

I'll Say, Say, Say what I want but don't
'spect you to run a fact-check
Take, take, take what you need, but don't
let Barry write a blank checque
All alone I'll sit there by the phone waiting for 3 a.m. (a.m.)
Through your ears how can you stand
to hear Obama's voters cheer?
You know I'm cryin' boo hoo hoo hoo hoo

Yeah

Go, go vote for who you want, But don't
you see that I'm more clever?
You, you, you say so long, but I've been campaigning forever
What can I do, now, to get through to you
'Cause I want to win it (win it)
Standing here baptized by Clinton years, baby through the years
You know I'm cryin' boo, hoo hoo hoo hoo

Ooh never ever worried, and I never shed a tear
You're sayin' that my words ain't real
Just look at my face, these tears ain't dryin'

You, you, you can never say that I'm not the one who earned it
I pray, pray, pray every day that you will listen well and learn it
What can I do, now to get through to you
'Cause I need to (need to) win it (win it)
Standing here baptised in all my tears, Survived Clinton years
You know I'm cryin', boo hoo hoo hoo hoo

Boo, hoo, hoo, hoo, hoo
Boo, hoo, hoo, hoo, hoo

It's Too Late
*Politicians make many excuses for their incredible statements.
I thought being 'sleep-deprived' was a good one.
Carol King's "It's Too Late" by (Fenslau/
Zimmermann/Katzmann/J. Stern/C. King)*

Stayed in bed all morning I was sleep deprived
There's something wrong here, there can be no denying
One of us sells Changing, but, Baby, I might start crying.

Is it's too late, Baby, now is it too late?
You know I really did try to make it
I spun that Bosnia Ride and I can't hide
I just tried to fake it.

It used to be so easy living there with Bill
Even though he's sleazy I could paddle through his swill
Now I am so unhappy, The Hill is like Jack and Jill.

And it's too late, Baby, now it's too late
'Cause Obama has legs to fake it
It's no swift-boat, it's lies that I can't hide
And he just might take it

There'll be bad times ahead for me and you
Taxes growing 'cross the nation, and you'll feel it too
Still I'm glad I still can do some more Senate Voodoo

But it's too late, Baby, it's too late
Though I really did try to make it
I spun the Bosnia ride and I can't hide
I just tried to fake it

John McCain

I'm John McCain, and I'm a RINO
Glen Campbell's "Wichita Lineman"

I am McCain and I'm a RINO
MSM says I'm gold
Everyone can see that my campaign
Is gonna be old

You'll hear me singing to the choir
And sometimes you'll hear me whine
For this John McCain RINO
Is doin' just fine

I know you fear some more taxation
And we'll lose all we've gained
And now that group that votes down south
Will carry John McCain

And you think that I'll betray us
And I'm cranky all the time
But this John McCain RINO
Is doin' just fine

Repeat chorus

All the Democrats will love me
'Cause with me their side will win
And this John McCain RINO
Is no Paladin

He's McVain
Carly Simon's "You're So Vain"

They talked about their Party
Like it was as easy as a chip-shot
Campaigns strategically dripped in rhetoric
They'd win it as like as not
They have both hands on our wallets as they take another shot
And all the candidates say they'll bring us
changes, life rearranges, and.

They're so vain, They don't think this vote is about you
They're so vain, I bet they think this isn't about you
Don't you? Don't you?

Well, I've watched them several years, you know,
And sometimes I've been naive
When they said that they'd bring us a brighter day
And Freedom would never leave
But they gave away the things I loved and wounded liberty
We had some dreams, but they sound just
like Kofi, Sound just like Kofi, and...

They're so vain, they don't care that this vote is about you
They're so vain, I bet they think this isn't about you
Don't you, Don't you?

Well I hear they went to the Michigan race,
And Romney (naturally) won
And now McCain is rising and no one knows
why we see this total eclipse of the sun
He's where he shouldn't be all the time
And when he's not he's there
Just poking our eye and with Ted he's a close
friend, Kerry's his close friend, and...

He's McVain, he probably thinks this game is about him
He's so Vain, I'll bet he thinks we all will elect him
Don't he Don't he?

(Repeat Chorus)
No McCain, we probably think you won't be our POTUS
What's to gain? We might as well surrender you've lost us
No Choice! No Voice!

Mistakes
"Escape" by Jimmy Buffett

I was tired of the campaign, it had gone on too long
Like a worn-out recording, of a tired old song
So while the good guys withdrew, I sat and shook my sore head
And in the silence of anger, this is the sound in my head.

If you hate Barack Obama, and getting kicked by McCain
If you're not into Clinton, cause you have half-a-brain
If you think our nation's fading fast, that it's bent out of shape
You need something to vote for, all the rest are mistakes!

I cannot think about the SCOTUS, I know that sounds kind of dim
But me and Grand Old Party, did not agree
to the things that drew me in
So I wrote to the party, Removed my name from their pad
And though I'm nobody's hero, I'm so glad that I have

"Yes, I hate Barack Obama, and getting kicked by McCain
I'm not into Clinton, 'cause I have half-a-brain
I think our nation's in a messy state, and it's bent out of shape
I need something to vote for, all above are mistakes.

So I moved on with no hope, who could I now support?
The GOP had betrayed me, who would now hold the fort?
I think I'll just write in Hunter, I know it won't get me far
And I'll cry for a moment, that they had to drop the bar

'Cause I hate Barack Obama, and getting kicked by McCain
I'm not into Clinton, cause I have half-a-brain
I think our nation's in a splintered state,
and the choices aren't great
It's the principle I'll vote for, all the rest are mistakes.

Dems are in Disguise
The Platters' "Smoke Gets in Your Eyes" by Otto Harbach/Jerome Kern

They asked me how I knew
John McCain was blue
I of course replied
Records he can't hide,
Cannot be denied

They said someday we'd fall
G.O.P.'s AWOL
When McCain's the guy
You must realize
Dems are in disguise

So I watched him and I shook my head
To think he could be the one
Now today, our hope has flown away
The GOP is done.

Now Obama is high
Our demise is nigh
So I smile and say
When McCain is the guy
Dems are in disguise!
G.O.P. has died.

No More Joy
The Shirelles' 'Soldier Boy"

No more joy
The MSM will end our joy
Now McCain's for you

You weren't my first choice
How can you be my last choice?
I will never vote for you
Ain't it true you're blue?
In the whole land
We could pick but one man
But it's just a real scam
The nod has gone to you

Your bid was over
But somehow you recovered
I don't believe
I can vote for you
You are a RINO
With Amnesty for forein-born
John McCain it is so true
I'll not vote for you

NO more JOY
MSM will now deploy
They'll be cruel to you.

Upside Down World
"Wonderful World" by Sam Cooke

Don't know much 'bout th'economy
Don't know much about honesty
Don't know why Conservatives are sick
Don't they know that I'm a Maverick?
But I do know I'm the nominee
And I know that if you vote for me
What an upside down world it would be.

I believe in pushing amnesty
Illegal aliens will vote for me
Closing GITMO is so right to do
Waterboarding? I'm against that too
But I do know that I'm your nominee
And I know that if you vote for me
What an upside down world it would be.

Now I don't claim to be an 'A' student,
Most my grades were Cs
But I was a prisoner, so don't you agree
You all owe this job to me?

Don't know much about ecology
Don't know much about biology
Never cracked open a science book
But I am a Global Warming kook
But I do know that I'll lean left
And although you all now feel bereft
What an upside down world this will be

Latatatatatatahuwaah (economy)
Oehwoewoe (amnesty)
Latatatatathuwaah (Science Book)
Oehwoewoe (Global Warming kook)

Only the Good Die Young
Billy Joel's 'Only the Good Die Young'

Come out Obama, don't make me wait
Your delegate count is just too great
Aw But sooner or later she'll fall to her fate
You might as well be the one

Well, You took on the Clintons, Told us to Hope
She isn't a racist but watch for the rope
Aw, but sooner or later you'll hit the downslope
For Hilly will be the one....
Only the good die young
That's what I said
Only the good die young (*X2*)

You might have heard she runs with a dangerous crowd
She ain't too pretty, she ain't too proud
She might be laughing a bit too loud
Aw But that never hurt no one

So come on Obama, show me a sign
Send up a signal I'll throw you a line
Those empty speeches your hiding behind
Things that you've never done
'Bama only the good die young
woah,I tell ya
Only the good die young (*X2*)

You got a nice white mom and your
party wants your confirmation
You come from Illinois mmmmm,
And you're no one's boy
But Obama they didn't give you quite enough information
You didn't count on Hill
Would take her aim on you with such ill will
(oh woah woah)

They say there's elections for those who will fight
Some say you'll win it, and I think you might
I guess I'll laugh at the lefties and cry with the right
'Cause John McCain ain't no fun...
You know that only the good die young
Oh woah baby, I tell ya
Only the good die young (X2)

You know that John McCain has not a
prayer of winning this election
Awww, He never tried to fight
When it was time for choosing wrong from Right
Oh woah woah

He's out, he's out, his election won't go his way
His right-wing cred came much too late
Sooner or later it comes down to age
He certainly ain't so young
You know that John McCain ain't the one!

I'm telling you baby
You know that only the good die young
Only the good die young
Only the gooooooooooooooood
Only the good die young
Only the gooooooooooooooood
Only the good die young
Oooooooooooooooooooooooo

McCain Ain't Right
Billy Joel's "You May Be Right"

Fright'ning night he crashed our party
The next day we felt so sorry
Others dropped and hopes were dashed again
He's from Arizona's sun
Wasn't hurting anyone
So the GOP selected John McCain

He's been stranded in a combat zone
Survived the Hanoi cell alone
Even though he's old we now have John McCain
And we told him not to run
'Cause his policies are dumb
And we said that only proves that they're insane.

(Refrain)
He might be Right, I may be crazy
But it's just a good conservative we're looking for
Turn out the light, don't try to change me
I may be wrong for all I know, but McCain ain't Right

Remember how he viewed the fence
With Feingold added more nonsense
And joined that nasty old gang of fourteen
We were looking for a man
He said take me as I am
'Cause you might enjoy a RINO on the team

Now think of all the years we tried to
Find someone who'd satisfy you
Bush might be as crazy as you say
If he's crazy then it's true
Then that RINO John is too
And we really don't embrace his Maverick ways.

(*Refrain*)
John may be Right, Bush may be crazy
But it's just a good conservative I'm looking for
Turn out the light, don't try to change me
I may be wrong for all I know, but McCain ain't Right

I may be wrong but McCain ain't right (*6x*)

I Get No Kick From McCain
"I Get a Kick out of You" by Cole Porter

I get no kick from McCain
Obama's gall doesn't thrill me at all
So tell me why should it be true?
That I get no kick from these two?

Some think that Barry's a gem!
Buy his audacious and hopeful refrain
But I don't buy that legerdemain
Cause he's even worse than McCain

I feel a kick every time I see them standing there before me
Right to the head though it's clear to see,
They obviously do not speak for me.

Some heed the words from the news
Bias and spin seek Obama to win
But tell me why should it be true?
When he spouts his shtick from the blue?

Some say that John's just too old
Why don't we fret that Obama's all wet?
So, Voters, please do as your told
Just kick out Obama, be bold!

Mack the Knife

One Townhaller ,thebigmick, calls McCain, Mack the Knife.
Bobby Darin's big hit "Mack the Knife" by
Kurt Weill & Bertolt Brecht-1928

Oh, McCain, Babe, has such teeth dear
And he shows us pearly whites
Just a jackknife has old McCain, Babe
And he keeps it...ah...out of sight.

Ya know when McCain stabs, with his knife, Babe
Scarlet billows start to spread
GOP Red, though, wears old McCain, Babe
But we'll never, never give him that cred.

Now on the campaign, uuh, huh, whoo...any morning' uuh,huh
Lies from Clinton and Obama spread...eek!
And someone's sneakin' 'round the corner
Could that someone be Mac the Knife?

A There's Obama..huh, huh, huh ...with
that anchor Reverend Wright
And that racist wag's just weighin' him down
Oh and Clinton is just, she's there for the race, dear
Five'll get ya ten the GOP will drown.

Now, d'ja hear 'bout that gang of fourteen? Old Johnny Mac, Babe
Campaign bill doesn't save our hard-earned cash
And old McCain spends just like a sailor
Could it be our boy's thrown conservatives in the trash?

Now ... border fences ... ho, ho ...yeah ...global warming
Ooh...Helps Illegal Aliens and puts Repubs down
Oh, the line forms on the LEFT, Babe
Now that Macky's , back in town.
Aah...I said Johnny Mac...whoa...He's so tawdry
Look out for Miss Hilly Clinton

and Obama Clown
Yes, that line forms on the Left, babe
Now that Macky's back in town.

Look out ... old Macky 's a hack!

Big John
Jimmy Dean's "Big John" by Johnny Cash

(Big John, Big John)
Ev'ry mornin' 'bout this time you will see him arrive
He's not very tall, so old he's barely alive
Kinda proud to be a maverick, and of his stay in Hanoi
And everybody knew we'd never feel no joy with Big John
(Big John, Big John) Big Bad John (Big John)

Nobody seemed to know how he won in the field
All the others dropped out and our blood just congealed
He didn't look strong, kinda puny in fact
His polls were down, how'd he get in the act, Big John?

Lately he's been raggin' on that place, New Orleans
Where he says that our government was lazy and mean
When that crashin' blow from a hurricane
Made him realize we had a need for McCain–Big John
(Big John, Big John) Big Bad John (Big John)

Then came that day, all the others stopped tryin'
And Old Huckabee fell and men started cryin'
We all were praying' and our hearts beat fast
And everybody knew our day was in the past, with John

Through the dust and the smoke of this man-made hell
Walked the shadow of a man that we all loved well
Grabbed our saggin' nation that we called home
And with humor and strength he just stood there alone–Big Ron
(Big Ron, Big Ron) Big Bad Ron (Big Ron)

And with all of his strength and by testing our will
He reminded us all we are a city on a hill
A shining beacon to a world in despair
And now he is gone, a memory's all we share of Big Ron

With tax and spending they've squandered our vote
Ripped our constitution with some new laws of note
Campaign funds and then that gang of fourteen
Everybody knew that soon he'd turn to green, Big John
(Big John, Big John) Big Bad John (Big John)

Now he's never believed in that worthless fence
Only in Iraq does he value defense
But these few words are written in the sand
A vote for John McCain will be the end of our land, Big John
(Big John, Big John) Don't Dig John (Big John)
[*Repeat and fade*]

I Am the Maverick!
From the hit song, "My Way" by Frank Sinatra,(P. Anka, J. Revaux, G. Thibault, C. Frankois)

Wake up, the end is near
Why don't you face the falling curtain
My friends, Election's here
I'll lose the race, of that I'm certain

I've lived a long long time
I've weathered much, and I'm no peacenik
But more, much more than this,
I've been a Maverick!

Regrets, I've had a lot
But what I've got, I will not mention
I've limped with what I've got
And will admit I'm no magician

I'm GOP perforce
Not really 'Right' if you must nitpick
I'm more than the dark horse
I am the Maverick!

Yes, there are times, I cross the aisle
And when I speak, how stiff's my smile?
But through it all, I know you doubt
That I know what I talk about
Although I'm slow, I think you know
I am a Maverick!

I've run, campaigned and tried
And against Bush, my fill of losing
I'll cross the great divide
And you won't find it amusing

To think I sought the nod
And made it stick, it warn't a cheap trick
Oh No, I'm no repub
I am the Maverick!

[Music swells]

For what is the Right, what has it got?
I won't be soiled by what they've wrought
I'll say the things I truly feel
And will not ride on Bush's heels
This prisoner knows, I took the blows
I am the Maverick!

He Has a Dopey Left Agenda
Hank Snow:" My Adobe Hacienda"

He has a dopey left agenda
Making friends with Mexico
Lacks the common sense of your kids,
Looming: Cinco de Mayo.
(Soft border guards and no fence is bizarre)
Brings more illegals to our streets
He has a dopey left agenda,
How can Dems we then defeat?

He has a dopey left agenda
When he speaks of Carbon Caps
That environmental nonsense
Only points out what he lacks
(Drills in ANWR would soon make him a star)
Sweet independence from Mid-East
He has a dopey left agenda,
Can't he do this Right, at least?

Joe Biden

It's Biden This Time

Well, I'm sorry that Obama didn't choose Bayh for his VP. It would have made a great bumper sticker: Bury Obama Bye! Oh well. Here's to the pick Biden, who once said the office of the President didn't lend itself to on-the-job training. Biden, who made a dismal showing among the potential Democrat candidates. I guess the other strong contenders are too problematic for Obama. Edwards managed to sully his reputation, and Obama doesn't have the courage to select Hillary. So much for trying to mend the party rift.

Here's an oldie. I'm Bidin' My Time. Not sure of the original authors, but it has been recorded by Judy Garland and featured in Crazy For You. I can hear Barack singing now:

It's Biden this time
'Cause he's the kinda guy I'm
While Clinton's in a tizzy
My Veep's hist'ry
Biden this time
Next year, next year
I'll be in the White House
This year, this year
No V.P. for Bill's spouse
'Cause it's Biden this time
'Cause we have articulate minds
There's no regrettin'
And I'm Bettin'
Biden's just fine
It's Biden this time
'Cause he's like the gaff-machine I'm
Where once he was complainin'
'Bout on-the-job trainin'
Biden this time
Next year, next year
This will all be history

This year, this year
Why he's here's a mystery
But it's Biden this time
'Cause he's the kinda guy I'm
No work outside the Senate
But he's no threat
Biden this time!

The Storybook Man

*Oh the irony in this quote! "I mean, you got the first mainstream African American who is articulate and bright and clean and a nice-looking guy. I mean, that's a storybook, man." —Joe Biden in January 2007
So, here is a parody to Sammy Davis Jr's hit song The Candyman.*

[Back ground music and Voters Sing
"Storybook! Hey, Storybook!"]
(Spoken) All right everybody, gather round, Storybook man's here!
What kind of promise you want? Healing the Ocean?
Sticking it to the Rich? Health care? Disarmament?
Anything you want! You've come to the right man!
Cause I'm the Storybook man!
Woooo!
Sings:
Who can make the sunrise?
Heal the oceans too?
Mix it up, he's chocolate, with a miracle or two
The Storybook,(the storybook) The Storybook
man (The Storybook man)
The Storybook man 'cause he shines like up above
And halos make him look good.
Who is like the Scarecrow?
Brainless or he's high?
Toke it up. The One's mistakes are really piling high
The Storybook (the storybook) The storybook
man (The storybook man)
The Storybook man 'cause no one can lay a glove,
And Biden makes him look good.
The Storybook man
Dazzling flim and flam
Falsifying and duplicious
Talk about his childhood wishes!
Everything he wrote's fictitious.

Who can fake tomorrow?
Spin it in a Dream?
Separate the voters and pretend he's all he seems?
A Storybook? (A Storybook) The storybook
man (The Storybook man)
The Storybook man 'cause his pay-scale's from above
He'll make us do what we should.
The Storybook man
Dazzling flim and flam
Falsifying and duplicious
Talk about his childhood wishes!
Everything he wrote's fictitious.
Who will cause us sorrow?
Carter warn't a dream!
Tax us all tomorrow til for energy we scream
A Storybook? (A storybook) The Storybook
man (The Storybook man)
The Storybook man 'cause when push comes up to shove
His plans we've misunderstood (We've misunderstood)
(*repeat and fade*)
Storybook! The Storybook! A Storybook

Ballad of Obama/Biden
The Ballad of Gilligan's Island (original by George Wyle and Sherwood Schwartz)

Just sit right back and you'll hear a tale
A tale of a fateful Lip
Who's welcomed as Obama's mate
But just wait for the 'trip'
The mate was a mighty Senator
Obama not so much
Two politicians on the stump
But we'll eat them for lunch, we'll eat them for lunch

The campaign started getting tough
Obama's compass lost
If he'd shown some courage and selected Change
He wouldn't look so soft, he wouldn't look so soft.

The Dems lost ground when Obama
named Joe Biden Denver-style
Not Hillary?
He skipped her too
Poor financiers! See his wife!
Peace protestors
The Election and Hope and Change
Hinge on Barry O's smile!

So this is the tale of Obama's day
He's stumped for a long, long time
He only makes a mess of things
It's an uphill climb.

Joe Biden and Obama too
Will do their very best
To sell snake-oil and be elect
If their tonic we ingest

No oil, no lights, no motor cars
Not a single luxury
Embracing Global Warming
Soon primitive as can be

So watch them now each week my friends
You're sure to get a smile
While the gaff-machine and Barry O.
Self-destruct in a while.

Tim Geithner

Call Me Indispensable
"Call Me Irresponsible" by: Cahn/Van Heusen
For Geithner (but it works for lots of Obama's appointments)

Call me indispensable
Though it's indefensible
I don't pay my taxes like you
Do my stupid alibis fool you?
Let me head the IRS
It's a SNAFU

Call me indispensable,
No tax for me liable
Cause it's undeniable you'll
Do as I say and not as I do

Sarah Palin

Sarah Sarah, Fills 'em with Terror
From the great shoo-op song, Donna, Donna, the Prima Donna by Dion and the Belmonts.

Sarah, Sarah, wearing Mascara Oh
Sarah, Sarah, girl for our Era Oh
Sarah, Sarah, needs a Tiara
Sarah, Sarah, fills 'em with Terror

Sarah, Sarah, fills 'em with Terror
Broke their heart
From the start
'Cause she's smart

We met a girl a week ago
We thought that John couldn't beat B. O.
But this time we realized
John grew a pair, no more disguise

I remember the Rights we hated
Always caving not complicated
Walking over our society
They all tried to make a fool out of me.

They call her Sarah, Sarah, Fills 'em with Terror
Broke their heart now
Cause she's smart now
From the Start now.

Pretty little girl on the campaign run
You're running all around and breaking Liberal hearts.
Pretty little girl, they don't stand a chance
We'll shout 'Barry, honey, there goes your romance'

Alaska has moose, salmon, oil galore
It's like our very own department store
She wants to free us from Loony Al Gore
Even shows grit to drill off-shore

They call her Sarah, Sarah, Fills 'em with terror
Broke their heart
'Cause she's smart
From the Start.
Pretty little girl on the campaign run
You're running all around and breaking Liberal hearts.
Pretty little girl, they don't stand a chance
We'll shout 'Barry, honey, there goes your romance'

Alaska has moose, salmon, oil galore
It's like our very own department store
She wants to free us from Loony Al Gore
Even shows grit to drill off-shore

Oh Oh Oh...
Sarah, Sarah, Fills 'em with Terror
(*repeat*)

It's Maverick!

On September 3, 2008, I wrote the following on my blog. "John McCain is starting to grow on me. My support was slow in gaining momentum, and on many issues I still disagree with him, but with his selection of Sarah Palin as his VP I am TOTALLY onboard with his ticket. I can never remember being so excited over a candidate for any office, and the hue and cry from the Left is so over the top it is even more delicious to observe! If the Main Stream Media had done even a rudimentary job of vetting, Obama would not be a presidential contender. In fact, I don't believe he could be qualified to get a Top Secret Clearance, based upon his mentors, friends and supporters."

Based on Pilot's It's Magic!

Ho, ho, ho,
It's Maverick! You know,
Never believe it's not so
It's Maverick, you know
Ever believe it is so!

Now it is a piece of cake
John has given us a break
Naming Sarah Palin with no warning!

Crazy days ahead
Music in my head
Lazy main stream media attacks her? Right!

Ho, ho, ho
It's Maverick, you know
I do believe it is so!
It's Maverick, you know
Ever I say "Way to go!"

I love her sunny ways
Dreams of better days
Dreaming of a landslide in the morning

John has been a Maverick
Palin just may do the trick!
Leftward bending willow John has seen the Light!

Ho, ho, ho
It's Maverick, you know
I do believe it is so!
It's Maverick, you know
Ever I say, "Way to go!"
(*Repeat chorus*)

Joy We're Expressing
From White Christmas, here is a remix of Irving Berlin's song," Counting My Blessings."

While I worried, and couldn't sleep
I count my blessings now Palin's the Veep
She's just what we seek!
Joy we're expressing.

When Obama was standing tall
I think that now his campaign will fall
And John' polls will leap!
Counting my blessings!

I think about our country and Obama surely dread
Now one by one discount him
As we vote for John instead.

If you're happy for John's great Veep
Just count your blessings we're No One's sheep
And Oh, what a Veep!
Joy, we're expressing!

I think about our country and Obama surely dread
Now one by one discount him
As we vote for John instead.

No more worries 'bout John's new Veep
A great selection, more votes to reap!
She's just what we seek!
Joy we're expressing!

Sarah-cuda!
Sarah Palin's nickname in school was Sarah
Barracuda. This is a natural!
Inspired! "Barracuda" by Heart

So this AIN'T the END!
John rises again! Today!!
I had to laugh so hard today!
Smiles like the sun!
This is for REAL!
E-Mails? - Watch Barry fail!

John flying so low under the dweebs
And now with Palin he is set free
Old Barry's down, down, down, down on his knees!
Look out dude!! Sarah-cuda!

Oh Oh.
Maverick this time isn't all wrong!
You see!
You found the purpose for me
No right is wrong, Sarah belongs!
Aflame,
We hear her name!

If the REAL thing don't do the trick
Dems better make up something slick
They're gonna burn burn burn burn down to the quick
OOOOHHHH! Sarah-cuda!
Oh oh!

Let me tell you Obama said
Dig down deep down to save my head
You! I think you got the blues too.

All last night I gave my best
Spoke without looking back
Made up some Marxist rules - silly fools!

If the REAL thing don't do the trick
Dems better make up something slick
They're gonna burn burn burn burn down to the quick
OOOOHHHH! Sarah! Sarah-cuda!
Ohhhhhhhh!

The Ballad of Palin's In
The theme from the TV show Have Gun will Travel!
'The Ballad of Paladin'
by Richard Boone, Johnny Western & Sam Rolfe

Palin's In, Palin's In, John's not alone
Palin's In, Palin's In, Hope for our Home!
Have Gun and Gavel Leads a Star with a Plan
"Good Night! Bye Obama" you're an average man
John's V.P. inspires; breathes a crushing wind
Our nation's good fortune Heed the cry of ....Palin's In!

Palin's In, Palin's In, John's not alone
Palin's In, Palin's In, Hope for our Home!
She'll travel onward! Conservative's Trust
A chess move delivers with a stab and thrust!
There are campaign legends that the newsmen spin
But they must be stunned
By the news that ...Palin's In!

Palin's In, Palin's in, John's not alone!
Palin's In, Palin's in, Hope for our home!
She's our own! She's our own!

WeWantObama2Lose

The GOP has a rising star in Sarah Palin. For a while she energized the McCain campaign and gave us hope that the election was not lost. Her selection as the VP running mate for McCain inspired the following. We need a website that says "WeWantObama2Lose!" from the Disney film, Cinderella: 'Bibbidi-bobbidi-Boo' (original by Verna Felton)

Since we got Palin,
Their son is failin'
WeWantObama2Lose
Put em together and what have you got?
WeWantObama2Lose!

She's from Alaska, Gibson would ask her,
Now Charlie looks like a fool
Put em together and what have you got?
WeWantObama2Lose!

Now we think the press is mean,
And they want McCain to lose
But the thing is the job
Will make Barry sob so
WeWantObama2Lose

Now that he's failin',
His tan is palin',
WeWantObama2Lose
Put it together and what have you got?

We want Obama to
We want Obama to
WeWantObama2Lose!

Nancy Pelosi

Kind of a Hag
Buckinghams Hit :"Kind of a Drag"

Kind of a hag, you know Pelosi's a pain,
Kind of a hag When Botox One is her plane
Oh She Won't Listen
(Listen to me when I'm speakin' 'cause you
know the things I'm thinkin')
To what you've got to say
('Cause I don't buy what she is diggin', Hope
and Change and bigger Piggin')
Nan's a Liberal
(Nan's a Liberal)
A Hate-America Liberal
(Hateful Liberal)
Everyday, Everyday!
Everyday!

Kinda of a Nag, When Barney Frank is the guy
When his finger wags, It really makes you wonder why?
Oh I can't listen
(Listen to me when I'm speakin' 'cause you
know the things I'm thinkin')
To that lisping he do
(And although he's on the bankers, we know he's a silly wanker)
No moral standing
(No moral standing)
For all his grand-standing
(All his Grand-standing)
Everyday, Everyday!
Everyday!

Oh Listen
(Listen to me when I'm speakin' 'cause you
know the things I'm thinkin')

To what they've got to say
(And although they give no reason, we
know that it's open season)
They are Rotten
(They're so rotten)
All Gains are ill-gotten
(They're misbegotten)
Everyday, everyday, everyday
[repeat and fade]

Pop Goes Pelosi
Watching Nancy Pelosi respond like a pop-up doll to every statement from Barack Obama inspired the following based on the familiar childrens' song that is often the tune cranked on a Jack In The Box toy.

Down and down
Obama's not Bush
His Hope and Change sounds cozy
Obama says that he is "the One"
Pop goes Pelosi

A billion for the new ship of state
A trillion for a bail-out
'Bama says it's just begun
Pop goes Pelosi

I'll fail you'll fail
It's all in the cards
Obama plays them daily
And all because he tells you "I won!"
Pop goes Pelosi

He signs a bill
The market tanks
But he says it's 'gyrations"
Don't you think his lying stinks?
Pop goes the Nation

Chapter Four:
Barack Obama

Born Me!

I am disturbed by Obama's arrogance. I can hear him sing the following. I think the authors' names for the original song are a happy accident!
Born Free by D. Black & J. Barry

Born Me! Which e'er way the wind blows,
I'll check where the poll goes
Born Me to Marxism start!

Lift Me, and Duty surrounds you,
My tax will astound as
You from your wallet I'll part!

Name Me and racists won't claim you,
You'll cast all the past aside
You'll soon embrace black pride!

Vote me, make my life worth living,
But only worth living
If you vote Me!!!!!

Call Me Obama
Artist: Billy Joe Royal's "Down in the Boondocks"

Call me Obama
Call me Obama
Hilly puts me down
'She wants to wear the crown
I was born to
I hate her, she hates me,
'cause I might interrupt her guarantee
Lord have mercy on the boy you-all call Obama.

Ev'ry night I dream about the White House and the Hill
I really want to go and live up there
And I guess I always will
But I'm the best man in this race
'Cause the Oprah is on my side
And all that Hill'ry Clinton has
Is her status as Billy's Bride

Call me Obama
Call me Obama
Hilly puts me down
She wants to wear the crown
I was born to
I hate her, she hates me
'cause I might interrupt her guarantee
Lord have mercy on the boy you- all call Obama.

Call me Obama
Call me Obama

One fine day I'll find a way to move from Illinois
I'll hold my head up like a king
And I ever will be filled with joy
Until November I'll work and slave
Campaignin' every dime

With the Oprah helping me be seen
Each night on Prime-time

Call me Obama
Call me Obama
Hilly puts me down
She wants to wear the crown
I was born to
I hate her, she hates me
'cause I might interrupt her guarantee
Lord have mercy on the boy you- all call Obama.
Lord have mercy on the boy you- all call Obama.
Lord have mercy on the boy you- all call Obama.

U Can't Touch This
MC Hammer's "U Can't Touch This"
Performed by M.T. Suit–you know the guy-

Can't touch this
Can't touch this
Can't touch this
Can't touch this
My, my, my, my campaign is just so hard
Oprah says,
Oh my Lord
Thank you for blessing me
With a man to run to set blacks free
He's good and I'll share my dough
He's a super-fine Senator from Chicago
And he's known as such
And here's a candidate, you can't touch
I say it with joy, can't touch this
Yeah, that's how I'm votin' and ya know,
Can't touch this
Look in his eyes man, can't touch this
Yo let me bust the next election, you can't touch this
Fresh hot,
I want romance
You know I really like him, gotta take a chance
So move him
Outta his seat
'Cause this Oprah girl, is so darn sweet
He'll be
Rollin' strong
Pump a little cash and you know what's going on
Like that,
Like that
O is on a mission, so just get back
Let 'em know I care too much
But this is just me uh they can't touch
Yo I told you, can't touch this
Think I'm a racist? Can't touch this
Yo sound the bell votes are in sucker

Can't touch this

Pandering votes, I'm with him
Money's no sweat that's what I'm gonna give him
Now you know
You talk about Obama what a row we're gonna hoe
That's hyped
Air tight
Obama is runnin' no stereotype
He is smart
Talks well
What's it gonna take for this package to sell?
With 'O'
Legit
We'll work so hard that the others will quit
That's word because you know
Can't touch this
Can't touch this
Break walls down!
(Oh-oh oh oh oh oh oh oh oh
Oh oh oh oh oh oh oh oh oh
Stop! He's Oprah's clown!
Go with Oprah it is said
If you don't think she's right then you probably are dead
So wave your hands with some joy
Vote Obama now get him outta Illinois
This is it, choose my winner
Listen to me and you know you'll get thinner
It's true
That he's black
Voting him for Prez is the greatest pay back
Vote, vote vote yeah, you can't touch this
Oprah says, you can't touch this
You know he'll be hyped boy 'cause you know you can't touch this
Cast your vote, let him in, O's in town!
Oh oh oh oh oh oh oh oh oh
Oh oh oh oh oh oh oh oh oh
Stop! Vote Oprah's clown!!

Hey Dude!
Beatles' "Hey, Jude"

Hey, Dude, Why are you sad?
Barack Obama will make it better
Remember he says he promises change
And only 'Change' will make it better

Hey, Dude, don't be afraid
Just because his mid-name's Hussein
The minute you let a doubt enter in
He cannot begin to make it better

And any time you feel the pain, hey, Dude, refrain
He'll carry the world upon his shoulders
Well don't you know that you're a fool to be his tool
He'll make this old world begin to smolder

Hey, Dude! Don't let him down
He says he Hopes Change will make it better
Remember, he only appeals to your heart
Then he can start, to make it better

So let it out, don't hold it in, hey Dude, begin.
He's waiting for someone to perform with
And don't you know that it's so true, hey Dude, You'll do
The movement he needs is on your shoulders

Hey Dude, Don't take it hard
It's a sad song, your cheeks are wetter
Remember he only appeals to your heart
Then he can start to make it better

Better, Better? Better??
Na-na-na-na-na-na-na, Na-na-na-na Na
You poor Dude! (*Repeats*)

You Gotta Have Hope
From Damn Yankees! "You Gotta Have Heart" Eddie Fisher

You've gotta have Hope!
All you really need is hope!
When Obama's saying he's gonna win,
His resume's thin-
But hope!

You gotta have Change!
Let him at the stock exchange.
Nuthin's half as hard as it may appear,
Just wait til next year
For Change

His experience is zero,
He has plans to take D C ,
Listen, he can be a hero
A little time and you'll see
There's nothin' to it 'cause he'll do it.

You've gotta be smart!
Miles and Miles and Miles of smart!
Don't you know he is a genius, of course,
But keep that old horse
Before the cart!
First, you gotta be smart!

Adams:
A great statesman, they haven't got!
Franklin:
A great diplomat, they haven't got!
Hale:
A great patriot, they haven't got!
All:
What've they got?

They've got HOPE!
All they really need is hope!
When those pundits tell them they'll never win,
That's when they will spin
You dope!

They've got Hope!
Why should GOPers Mope?
But you see the final inning remains
And look for some change
And Hope!
We're not happy that he's runnin'
But the hopeful thing to do
Is to know our ship will come in
So, it's ten years overdue!

We've got heart
Miles, and Miles and Miles of heart
Oh we wish we had a genius, of course
But keep that old horse
Before the cart

So what the heck's the use of cryin'?
And why should we curse?
We know things gotta get better
Because they couldn't get worse!

And to add to it
We've got Hope!
We've got Hope!
We've got Hope!

Let Barack Take You Away!
Steppenwolf, "Magic Carpet Ride"

He likes to dream
yes, yes
And what he says is the new theme
On a cloud of hope he drifts in the night
Any place he'll go but right
Fans scream, cry tears, he's a star, no one could fear

Well, you don't know what he might hide
Says he "Just come with me little world
On my magic carpet ride.
You don't know what I can see
Why don't you sell your dreams to me
Fantasy will set us free
Close your mind world
Step aside world
Let Barack take you away!"

Last night he held back Clinton's camp
And no one wished that she would stay
Before Barack could sew things up
Someone messed the whole thing up!
He looked around, they both are nomination bound.

Well, you don't know what's left to find
Why don't you look and see little world
I've got magic on my side.
Well, you don't know what I can see
Why don't you sell your dreams to me
Fantasy will set us free
Close your mind world
Just stay blind world
Let Barack take you away!

Why Obama?
By the Knack, "My Sharona"

Oh now listen everyone, Everyone
When you gonna tell us the truth, Obama?
Ooh you're on your campaign run,
Campaign run
Running on the new party line, Obama
Say you're giving Hope,
Give it up
But what's on your mind?
Clintons should give up
To the rush of the younger kind,
My My My I Yi Woo.
M M M My! Obama?

Look a little closer huh,
Ah will ya huh?
Close enough to look at his lies, Obama?
Keeping him a mystery
Gets to me
Running on the strength of his ties, Obama
Never gonna stop,
Give it up,
But what's on his mind?
Must we give it up
For the touch of the wunderkind?
Why Why Why I Yi Woo!
W W W Why Obama?

When's he gonna shaft you and me,
You and me?
Is it just a matter of time? Obama?
Is it just destiny,
Destiny?
Or is this just a fear in my mind, Obama?
Never gonna stop,

Won't give up,
Say what's on your mind?
I won't give it up
'Til we hear why we must be blind.
My My My I Yi Woo.
B B B Bye Obama
Just say Goodbye, Obama.
B B B Bye Obama!

Back Home to Chicago
From the Blues Brothers, "Sweet Home Chicago"
original lyrics by Robert Johnson

Come On
Oh Baby can you see that show?
Come on
Oh Baby don't you want to know?
Barack sent Jeremiah Wright
Back home to Chicago

Come on
Don't you think he has a case?
He Say
He never heard that stuff befo'
Now Jeremiah's not to show his face
Outside of Chicago

Well, one and one is two
Six and two is eight
Add 'em all together and I think you'll see straight
Hidy-hey
Don't you think Obama knows?
Race is just there for bait
Back home in Chicago

Come on
Don't you think Obama knows?
Race is just there for bait
Back home in Chicago

Six and three is nine
Nine and Nine is eighteen
Twenty years in common, now you know what I mean!

Hidy-hey
Don't you think Obama knows?
That his church espouses hate?
Back home in Chicago

Oh come on
Don't you think Obama knows?
Come on
Don't you think Obama knows?
Send him back in disgrace
To his home in Chicago.

Globama
Original words by Lilla Cayley Robinson, modern words by Johnny Mercer and Music by Paul Lincke) "Glowworm"

Shining black Obama, 'bama
Son of a white Mama, Mama
Can we trust his face we wonder?
Is it just his race we ponder?
Shine Obama, glimmer, glimmer
Although your star is getting dimmer
Take a stand for love and hope
Obama you're no dope

Glow Obama, man of races
Why should we worry you've two faces
Defeat the female of the Demos
You've got the message and the Memos
Your star could use a little brightnin'
"Cause Reverend Wright is pretty frightnin'
When you gotta glow, you glow
Tell us what we should know

How will you fix the damage, he caused?
No one believes you missed it, because
If he's your so-called spiritual mentor
How can we think you'll take the center?
In this election season, season
Nothing has any rhyme or reason
We don't need more vitriol
Look to your nation's soul

Now we've all heard your Hope 'n Audacity
There's not a doubt you have tenacity
You don't see Wright as a racist
But say your grandma has that basis
See how the campaign starts to darken
But to your voice the people hearken

Just say the word and they will scream
Dream Obama Dreams

One more pass to keep momentum
Brokered conventions happen seldom
Just tell us all to stop and ponder
Clinton will not make us fonder
Don't worry Barry you can lick it
Ignore the facts now, that's the ticket
Just keep telling us to hope
That you're not a misanthrope

No Thicket to Hide

I wrote this one because of the story told by Uncle Remus about Brer Rabbit. Brer Rabbit tricked his captors by convincing them that to toss him into the briar patch was a fate worse than death. (Of course, the briar patch was home, so saying the opposite got him tossed exactly where he wanted to be!) Sometimes I get the impression Obama would like to employ the same kind of mis-direction.
Beatles' "Ticket to Ride."

I think it's gonna be bad
I think it's today, yeah
The candidate that we had
Is slippin' away

(*Chorus*)

He's got no thicket to hide
He's got no thicket to hide
He's got no thicket to hide
And I don't care.

He said that listening to Wright
Was just the Black sound, yeah
How could he think it was right?
I think that's profound.

(*Chorus*)

I know that he was ridin' so high
He ought to think twice
He ought to do right you see
And now there's voters saying goodbye
He ought to think twice
He ought to do right you see?

I think the world is gone mad

I think it's today, yeah
Obama has to be sad
Wright gave him away, yeah.

(*Chorus*)

I know that he was ridin' so high
He ought to think twice
He ought to do right you see
And now there's voters saying goodbye
He ought to think twice
He ought to do right you see?

Michelle said into the crowd
(It's bringing him down, yeah)
That she had never been proud
Of our U.S.A.

They've got no thicket to hide
They've got no thicket to hide
Now they've got no thicket to hide
And I don't care!
I really don't care.
I really don't care (*repeat*)

Pay It Back
The Rolling Stones' "Paint it Black"

Barack Obama says his race is only black
No White relations 'cause he wants to be called black
You see he doesn't want to walk in Whitey's shoes
He must identify himself, or he might lose

I listen to a preacher who is screaming hate
He's wearing fancy clothes as he gesticulates
I see the people rise and shout all their bodies sway
But Barry won't disown this hatred on display.

I look inside the church and wonder is it 'black?'
I see my nation and I hear them talking smack
I hope this fades away and we can just face the facts
There's not a chance for change when it is 'white' or 'black'

No more will I believe this nation should be blue
I hate these liberal lies that racists think are true
If you look hard enough you might discern the lies
But will Obama shed this awful racist guise?

He sees our nation and he wants to take it back
Soon reparations will be in his taxing sack
I don't believe he has the audacity of hope
I have to just believe he thinks we all are dopes!

Hmmmm Hmmmm Hmmmm

He wants us to be paying, paying back
Black is might, black his soul
He wants to see that we cannot argue his choice
He wants to see us paying, paying, paying, paying back!
Yeah!

Say I Have Audacity
Original song, "Call Me Irresponsible" by: Cahn/Van Heusen

Say I have audacity
Say it's perspicacity
Throw out it's mendacity too!
Do my foolish alibis bore you?
Well I'm just a Senator
But, I want more, dude!

Say I am articulate
Black folk I'll emancipate
Rainbow Coalition pursue
Tell me it's implausible,
That Wright wasn't audible
But it's undeniably true
I've the audacity to fool you.

Ain't Never Had a Friend Like Me
At the request of LOLO1, I did the following parody from Aladdin. I can almost hear Barry singing it! "You Ain't Never Had a Friend Like Me" Alan Menken & Howard Ashman

Now the Senate has more than forty thieves
And Ms Pelosi tells a thousand tales
But Massah you in luck 'cause up my sleeve
I got a brand of magic never fails
I got some power in my corner now
The heavy ammunition's in my face
I've got some punch, pizzazz, yahoo and how
See all I gotta do is play my race
And I'll say:

Just trust Obama, sir
What will your pleasure be?
Let me take your order
Jot it down
You ain't never had a friend like me
No no no

I am your candidate
Just put your trust in me
C'mon whisper what it is you want
You ain't never had a friend like me

Yassah,
I'll bring them to the table
Negotiate
With kings, and shahs
Ask what you wish
I'll serve their dish
How about a little more Baklava?

I'll raise the income tax
Health care for all, you'll see
I'm in the mood to help you dude
You ain't never had a friend like me

Can McCain do this?
Can Clinton do that?
I'm gonna pull it all out of my little...hat!

I'll make them all go Poof!
Well, looky here
I'll just go Abracadabra, let 'er rip
And then make them suckers disappear!
So don't ya sit there slackjawed, buggy eyed
I might just institute some midday prayers
A liberal bonafide, certified
I'm gonna raise the roof y'old taxpayers
I got a powerful urge to help you out
So Whatcha wish? I really wanna know
I've got a list that's three miles long, no doubt
Well all you gotta do is vote like so, and oh!

I'm just Obama, sir, I'll grant a wish or two or three
I want the job, I'm your heart-throb
You ain't never had a friend, never had a friend
You ain't never had a friend, never had a friend
You ain't never had a friend like me
You ain't never had a friend like me, hah!

When You Catch Obama's Star
*I guess I hear voices a lot! I can almost hear
Jiminy Cricket singing this one!
The Oscar-winning song from "Pinocchio" by Leigh
Harline "When You Wish Upon a Star."*

When you catch Obama's star
Makes no difference who you are
Anything your heart desires
He'll say to you

If you listen to his dreams
You will see he's too extreme
When you catch Obama's star
As Liberals do

Change your mind
He comes not from above
No sweet fulfillment of
Our secret longings

Like a dolt out of the 'Blue'
He steps in with 'change,' you fool
No more wishing on his star
Lest 'change' comes true

Obama (Tin Man)
From "Tin Man" by America.

Sometimes lately I appeal
To those who share the gift of gab between themselves
Some are quick to take the bait
And set Barack Obama high upon a shelf

Because no one wants to challenge B. Obama
'Cause he isn't, isn't just really bad
Because no hard-hitting questions for Obama
Makes him look like he's Sir Galahad

So please believe in me
When I say he's spinning round, round,
round round
Smoke and mirrors, color
Image going down, down, down, down
Wright and race give troubles

Oh 'cause no one wants to challenge B. Obama
'Cause he might not, might not give any hope
And 'cause never was the reason for believing
Just the topic of why he's a joke

So please believe in me
When I say they're spinning, round, round, round, round
Smoke and mirrors, color
Image going down, down, down, down
Wright and race give troubles

Oh, 'Cause no one wants to challenge B. Obama....*(repeat)*

Razzle Dazzle

It makes me think of the scene from the movie Stripes when Bill Murray and the motley crew of mis-fits do 'razzle dazzle' on the parade ground. Was it impressive? They faked it beautifully! That's what I think of Obama: no experience, and he fakes it a lot. Maybe he should add a tap-dance to his campaign? I have my favorites. This is one of them.
From Chicago: "Razzle, Dazzle" by John Kander & Fred Ebb

Give 'em the old razzle dazzle
Razzle Dazzle 'em
Give 'em an act with lots of race in it
Just go ahead and rub their face in it
Give 'em the old hocus-pocus
Bait and switch-y 'em
They won't believe what they see with their eyes.
Ignore the hate your friends are gushing!
What if, in fact, they're just disgusting?
Razzle Dazzle 'em
And they'll never catch wise!

Give 'em the old Razzle Dazzle
Razzle Dazzle 'em
Give 'em the plan that's so splendiferous
Tax after tax will grow a gift fer us
Give 'em the old flim flam flummox
Fool and pander 'em
Why should they seek the truth above the roar?
Throw out some hope and more audacity
Stretch all the lies beyond capacity
Razzle Dazzle 'em
And they'll beg you for more!

Give 'em the old double whammy
Tax and Spend-ium
You can propose a referend-ium
Top it all off with free health care fer 'em

Give 'em the old three ring circus
Fluff and Flatter 'em
When you're in trouble, just say you mis-spoke
Although they say you're so articulate
"Punished with babies" seems an epithet
Razzle dazzle 'em
Send in mirrors and smoke

Give 'em the old Razzle Dazzle
Bamboozle 'em
Show 'em the cut-rate Senator you are
Just keep your head and then remember son
Hoodwink 'em all until November's won
Razzle Dazzle 'em
And they'll make you a star!!!

ALTERNATE VERSE (**adult content**):

Give 'em the old Razzle Dazzle
Look down on 'em
Why not reveal the demagogue you are?
When you portray us all as bitter
That's when we see you're a bull-shitter
Razzle Dazzle 'em
And they'll make you a star!!!!

Mudcat, Mudcat

Mary Katherine Hamm wrote an article about the democratic strategist whose nickname is Mudcat. So here is a song for Obama asking Mudcat for some assistance!
"Muskrat Love" by America

Mudcat, Mudcat, lend your aid
Barry Obama is so afraid
That he blew it
And you-all knew it

Mudcat, Mudcat set him straight
Most of his friends are not that great
Some of them racists
Or terrorist faces

And he's spinnin' his words in a tangle
Looking for a better angle
Looks like he's swampin' his boat
Can't he just hold onto his hope?

Mudcat, Mudcat
Handle th' fight
Lovin' small towns and hatin' the right
But Obama
Ads to the drama

Small-town Susie, Red-neck Sam
All those litterbugs out in Small-town land
They're just bitter
Like Abe the Rail-splitter

And now he's asking for Mudcat to come save the day
Barry's afraid he will fade away
Says he's audacious!
But, Oh Goodness Gracious!

Now he's spinning his words in a tangle
Looking for a better angle
Don't you think he's missing the boat
But he's counting on his hope to float!

Obama (Cecilia)
This was written at the end of April when Hillary's campaign took on a last minute surge.
From Paul Simon & Art Garfunkle's "Cecilia."

Obama, you're breaking apart
You're shaking our confidence daily
Oh Obama, You say what you please
But you're just a sleaze, so go home
Obama, You're just and upstart
You're faking your campaigning daily
Oh Obama, It's not about race
No Crystal Staircase, just go home
Go on Home.

Hawking hope in the afternoon: It's Obama,
But there's pending doom. (yes, there is!)
Soon to Hill he'll lose his place
'Cause at heart the campaign's
About gender and race.

Obama, you're hangin' with Wright
And Ayers' Weather Underground daily
Oh Obama, You want us to vote
You're bankin' on hope, but go home
Go on Home.

Jubilation, now Clinton's redeemed
We all see the fall and we're laughing
Jubilation, She's picking up steam
Obama will fall and we're laughing
Oh Oh Oh Oh, Obama will lose
Who else can we choose
Maybe Hilly!
Oh Oh Oh Oh, Obama will lose
Old Chaos is loose
What sensation!
Oh Oh Oh Oh (fade)

Obama (La Bamba)
It was inevitable. From Richie Valens' hit "La Bamba"

What do you say Obama?
What do you say Obama
About the trouble your campaign is having?
Troubles you might deny but you cannot hide
You keep playing the race card
You keep playing the race card its charms to ride
its charms to ride
its charms to ride

You were dissed by Ferraro
You were dissed by Ferraro
A Democrat
A Democrat
A Democrat
Bama, Bama
Bama, Bama
Bama, Bama

What do you say Obama?
What do you say Obama
When you are not able to beat Mrs. Clinton?
Close the gap upon Clinton and you can win
But El Rushbo makes Chaos
(guitar)
You are not a straight arrow
You are not a straight arrow
You hang with Wright and Ayer's Weather Underground
Weather Underground & Wright will bring you down
And you cannot deny them
They are both a part of your campaign run
It can't be done.
It Can't be done.
Bye, Bye, Bama
Bye Bye, Bama
Bye Bye, Bama

Baa Baa Black Sheep

From the nursery rhyme song "Baa Baa Black Sheep" Is Obama a wolf in sheep's clothes?

Baa Baa Black Sheep
Are you just naive?
No sir, no sir I don't believe.
Once you were hopeful, now you are lame
Now the best we hope for is 'lose with McCain'
Bah Bah Black Sheep
Is it just your race?
No sir, we just think you're a disgrace!
Why should we think that you see Wright as wrong?
When for those twenty years you just went along?
Bah Bah Black Sheep
We can see beneath
We don't believe your smile doesn't have any teeth!
'Punished with Babies' seems a bit extreme
But your voting record does justify this meme.
Bah Bah Black Sheep
You won't get my vote!
Too bad alternatives don't hold any hope.

Pirouettes on the Stage

I loved it when President Bush made a general statement of USA policy while visiting the middle east, and Obama immediately expressed offense. Might we assume this was his first 'pre-emptive strike' in his campaign? Guilt is a funny thing, isn't it? So, for Obama, who wants to sit down and talk with our enemies. This is even funnier when you realize that his Chief of Staff, Rahm Emanuel, was once a ballet dancer! I expect more pirouettes to come.

From Herman's Hermits' hit song: "Silhouette on the Shade" -Frank C. Slay Jr. & Bob Crewe

[background singers: "Pirouettes, pirouettes, pirouettes on the stage"]

Look, I listened to George Bush
Late last night
All my aids were tired and drawn
So up-tight
But that speech from Israel
Said we'd not appease Iran
Nor any other terrorist regime

I was sure he spoke to me
I was sore
So I thought I would deny
What I said before
There's no doubt that I'm the guy
Who's DNAs on that claim
What could I do?
I can't be called Chamberlain.

Ah-ah-ah-ah-ah....

Lost control and found a mike
I was sore
No one else can pin that tripe
At my door
Old George Bush can just refrain

From dragging around my name
Said to my staff
I'll make a pre-emptive strike!

Made a case that he was wrong
Me Appease?
Don't you say that about me
If you please!
I won't be the one so, Jeez
Just forget I am naive
I only said, I'd talk to our enemies!
(*Background singers repeat: "Pirouettes."*)
Ah-ah-ah-ah-ah....

Oh Obama!
'Oh Susanna' (Stephen Foster)

I come from South Chicago with some Mojo don't ya see?
I'm goin' to win the White House, cause 'most everyone loves me
Campaigned all night, they say I'm Left
But magic's in my eyes
My run's so hot you can't believe
Obama's not your guy

I'm Obama, y'all must vote for me
I come from south Chicago
with my Mojo don't ya see?

I had a dream the other night
When everything was still
I thought I saw old Reverend Wright
A swearing next to Hill
A racist rant was in his mouth
A tear came to her eye
Said I, You'd better shut your mouth
Obama's not your guy

I'm Obama, y'all must vote for me
I come from south Chicago
With my Mojo don't ya see?

He soon will be in the White House
And then you'll look all 'round
That's when you'll link Obama,
With Weather Underground!
But if you don't elect him
This darkey'll surely die
His campaign dead and buried,
Obama's not your guy!

Oh! Obama, you do not speak for me
Though you come from South Chicago
Magic Mojo I don't see.

I'm a Clown

*Cole Porter's song "Be A Clown" You know this one
if you've ever seen the movie Singin' in the Rain.
Of course, Obama is no Donald O'Connor.*

We'll recall his campaigning
Fresh from Illinois
'Bama, Prez in Training
Must be the best boy
He said, when I grow up
I want to be Prez
I want my future sewn up
But everyone says:

I'm a clown, I'm a clown
Bozo's come to our town
I'm a fool, king of gaffs
Who knows who'll have the last laugh?
Wear a smile, with Michelle
They'll faint when the rhetoric swells
If I dismiss my blunders, folk'll just shake their head
If I dismiss those pundits, they'll just play Wright instead
If it would get me delegates I'd stand on my head
I'm a clown, I'm a clown, I'm a clown.

I'm a clown, I'm a clown
Bozo's come to your town.
They don't see a buffoon
That's why the voters all swoon.
Wear a pin, touch your heart
Don't you know that Barry is smart?
For Hamas and Al Qaeda, I have an embrace
They say that if I talk to them it's just a disgrace
But I am sure I'll never ever fall on my face
I'm no clown, I'm no clown, I'm no clown!

I'm no clown, I'm no clown
All you guys settle down
Show 'em smiles, tell 'em naught
Don't they know I'm the answer they sought?
I'm a crack jackanapes
Darwin says: descended from apes
Why be a great Orator? When I show up there's cheers
I think I can maintain this act for maybe four years
But don't you think they'd giggle if I wiggled my ears!
I've renown, I've renown, I've renown!

I've renown, I've renown,
All the world sees my crown
If I just make 'em vote
I'll deflect those lobs from swift boats
Speak of Ayers, confess dope
Throw in audacity: Hope
A college education from old Harvard, my friend
A college where it surely was a boost to attend
What a hoot to be the President in the end
I've renown, I've renown, I've renown!

Simmer down! Simmer down!
Soon I'll own Tinseltown
I'm as bright as the sun
Soon I'll climb aboard Air Force One
Cling to God, hold your guns
Wait until you see my end run
If you are midwest farmers, you fight weather and luck
But fixing global warming will make everything suck
So Jack just pay the taxes, here I won't stop the buck
I'm no clown, I'm no clown, I'm no clown!

Talk to Our Enemies
From Dr. Doolittle's "Talk to the Animals" by Leslie Bricusse

If we could talk to our enemies
Just imagine it
Chatting with Hamas or Old A.Q.
Imagine Syria with dinner
Who would be the winner?
What a neat achievement! Wouldn't you?

If Barry talks to the terrorists
Learns their languages
Maybe even he could someday see
That Afghans do not speak like Arabs
Iran needs a rehab
Why he'd make us guinea pigs, you see?

And old Al Gore says polar bears are dying
So we'll reverse our thermostats and freeze
If people asked, "Is this the way to save our place?
We'd say, "It's a disgrace! Heat please!"

If we just bow to our Liberal friends'
'Man from animals'
Think of all the things we could discuss
If we could Talk like a liberal
Wink like a liberal
Think and Blink, be Finks like a Liberal
And they could talk until the Missing Link is us!

I'm an Appeaser
Original "I'm a Believer" by Neil Diamond

I thought running for the Prez was fairy tales
Meant for only Whites and not for me
Bush was out to get me
That's the way it seemed
Then I hit the stage and voters screamed!

Then you saw my face, now I'm an appeaser
Not a trace of doubt in my mind
I tell you Gov, I'm an appeaser
Not an old Geezer, like McCain

I think that the USA should give some bling
Seems the more you give the less you got
What's the use in tryin'?
I'll beat John McCain
Global Warming sanctions cause you pain?

But just see my race, I'm an appeaser!
Not a trace of doubt in my mind
It's all love, I'm an appeaser
Just a bull-squeezer, where's my spine?

I Saw A Candidate!
From 'Witch Doctor' by Ross Bagdasarian

I saw a candidate
I don't think he's so great!
I saw a candidate
I think he is a snake!
I saw a candidate
He told me how to vote, he told me:
Ooo Eee Oo Ah Ah Bing Bong I'm Obama Ding Dong! (*X4*)

I told the Democrats
I didn't like his roots
I told the Democrats
With Wright he's in cahoots
And then the Democrats they said 'twas time to choose
They told me
Ooo Eee Ooo Ah Ah Ting Tang He's Obama bing bang (*X4*)

(*Bridge*)

He's been selling hope to me just like a politician
And I'll admit that he seems very smart
So when I looked the GOP had altered their position
And that's not the way for them to win my heart

My friends, the GOP
They think that John's the guy
My friends, the GOP
They spit right in my eye
So, Friends, I think it's true
I will not vote for you
And I say:
Ooo Eee Oo Ah Ah Ding Dang All those
Silly RINOs Cause Pain! (*X4*)
(*Repeat last verse and refrain*)

Obama, Naturally

I wrote this after Obama's Memorial Day speech when he 'saw' the honored heroes in the audience. Someone needs to clarify for him the difference between Memorial Day and Veteran's Day.
Addams Family Theme (Vic Mizzy)

He's creepy and he's spooky
Delirious and goofy
He's altogether stoop-id
Obama, Naturally

When speaking for Memorial
Did he sound Senatorial?
He needs a new tutorial
Obama, Naturally

[Gaffe]
[Chaff]
[He's Daft!]

So while he is campaigning
Where did he get his training?
He's losing all he's gaining.
Obama, Naturally

<click> <click>

That Oh! Obama Spell

"That Old Black Magic" by Johnny Mercer and Harold Arlen. This one is for Ann Coulter, who reminded us of the 'tingles' Chris Matthews gets when he sees Obama.

That Oh! Obama has them in his spell
With the same old stories Jesse Jackson tells
Those old left-wingers that can't find their spine
That guy Obama-Chris says is sublime

The same old tingle as we start the ride
And then that roller-coaster starts to glide
And down and down we go, round and round we go
And we have nowhere else to hide

He should fade away, but what can we do?
They hear his name; there's more acclaim!
A man with such a need to appease
Can't we just find better candidates, please?

Is he the savior we've been waiting for?
The POTUS that this land was slated for?
But every time his lips opine,
Darling....

Down and down we go,
Round and round we go
He's a clown, he needs a dressing-down,
I wish that Oh! Obama'd step down.

We Don't Like B.O.

Speaking of Spells...here's one to spell it out.
From the children's song: B-I-N-G-O!

There's a Candidate who made a gaffe
And B.O. is his name-oh
We Don't Like B.O.
We Don't Like B. O.
We Don't Like B. O.
And B.O. is his name Oh

There's a Candidate, a real Bozo
and B.O. is his name-oh
(Clap) Don't like B. O.
(Clap) Don't like B. O.
(Clap) Don't like B. O.
And B.O. is his Name-Oh

He's an appeaser and that's true
And stinks just like B.O.-oh
(Clap, clap) Like B.O.
(Clap, clap) Like B.O.
(Clap, clap) Like B.O.
And stinks just like B.O.-Oh

He says we don't need God or Guns
'Cause Hope will overcome-oh
(clap, clap, clap) B.O.
(clap, clap, clap) B.O.
(clap, clap, clap) B.O.
'Cause hope will overcome-Oh

When he is oval office-bound
We, in despair will say-Oh
(clap, clap, clap, clap) OH
(clap, clap, clap, clap) OH
(clap, clap, clap, clap) OH
We Didn't Want that B.O.

Obama, No!
Van Morrison's "Domino"

I think we'd discuss it!
I don't buy his call for change
You may get disgusted
And think I'm strange
Hangin' out with Weather Underground
Wright and all the rest
Never has he worried
About what is worst and what is best

Oh, Obama, no!
Poll me over oh no no
There you go
Lord have mercy
I said Oh, Obama no!
Poll me over oh no no
There you go
Say it again
I said oh Obama no
I said Oh Obama no

He's a phony candidate
He's no candidate at all!
And all that you will hear from him
It's just Hope he'll make the call
Or vice versa
Votes depend on where ever you're at
And if he never hears from me
That just means I would rather not

I said, Oh Obama No.
Poll me over oh no no
There you go
Lord have Mercy
I said Oh, Obama, no

There you go
Say it again
I said oh Obama no
I said Oh Obama no!

Who's a Bully?
Didn't you just love Sam the Sham and the Pharaohs?
Here's 'Wooly Bully' by Domingo Samudio

Uno, dos, one, two, Nine-Eleven
[Hey! Who's a bully? Watch it! They're gone,
They're gone, Watch it now!]

Ahab told A-jab
About those guys they hate
Then came B.O. to Negotiate
Who's a bully? Who's a bully?
Who's a bully? Who's a bully? Who's a bully?

Ahab told A-jab
"Let's don't take no chance'
Remember Nine Eleven
They will learn our dance"
Who's a bully? Who's a Bully?
Who's a bully? Who's a bully? Who's a bully?
[watch it now, watch it watch it!]

(*Sax Riff & scream*)

Ahab told A-jab
"That's the thing to do.
They'll get B. Obama
To play the fool for you."
Who's a bully? Who's a bully?
We're a bully? We're a bully? We're a bully?
[Watch out! Watch it now, Take Off!]

Knick-Knack Paddy Whack!
From the children's song, 'This Old Man.' Gotta Love a song with your name in it!

B.O. man, he plays one
He plays knick-knack and he's dumb
With a knick-knack, whack Iraq
Bring the soldiers home
Is his head just solid bone?

B.O. man, he plays two
He plays knick-knack, now we're screwed
With a Knick-knack, whack Iraq
Give Iran a bone
B.O. wants the soldiers home.

B.O. man, he plays three
Is his mind just 'absentee?'
With a knick-knack, whack Iraq
Give A.Q. a bone
B.O. wants the soldiers home

B.O. man, he plays four
Immigrants get revolving doors
Not a kick-back, Send 'em back
Use a microphone
Can't we send illegals home?

B.O. man, he plays five
Thinks dead soldiers are alive
With a knick-knack, what a hack
Give Matthews a bone
Why should his gaffes stand alone?

B.O. man, he plays six
Thinks that Reverend Wright's a pip
With a knick-knack, holler back

BLT 's his crowd
B.O. has a wife who's proud

B.O. man, he plays seven
Does he remember nine-eleven?
With a knick-knack, we fought back
But B.O. is sure
Hope will keep us safe right here

B.O. man, he plays eight
Weather Underground's not great!
With a knick-knack, listen Jack
Terrorists are bad
Look at all the friends he's had

B.O. Man, he plays nine
He says Change will be sublime
With more kick-backs, some for Blacks
Reparations soon?
B.O. needs a better tune.

B.O. man, he plays ten
He's Jimmy Carter o'er again
With a knick-knack, whack Iraq
Sit down with A-jad
He's our U.S.A. jihad.

The Men Who Vote: Barry Obama
'The Man Who Shot Liberty Valance,' Burt Bacharach

When Barry Obama rode into town the voters saw his pride, his pride
When Barry Obama talks about the things he wants to try
But if clinging to God and to Guns is wrong,
What else don't Barry get?
When it comes to taxes, and the terrorists, both big ears are wet!

From out of his church a preacher came, the
Good Book in his hand, a man
The kind of a man to stir up hate within a troubled land
But a rule made of gold was among the laws
that preacher mis-understood
When it came to honor U.S.A....that preacher was no good.

Many a fool could seek my vote, and many a fool would fall
The men who vote: Barry Obama, that vote: Barry Obama
They are the stupidest of all.

The love of acclaim can make a man stay
on when he should go, go on
And claimin' he has as much experience as anyone
But the hope in our hearts cannot hide the
side where Marxist Barry stands
When it comes to choosing right from left, the nation's in our hands.

Alone and afraid I pray that we our nation's
course can right, awwww upright!
When nothing we say can keep our
freedoms, Gracie, say 'Goodnight!'
From the moment the left gets to be full-
blown the very first thing we know
When no one makes the case for sovereignty,
Welcome Mexico-O-O-Oh.

Everyone has a vote for life, a life in Liberty's Hall
But the men who vote, Barry Obama, Who'll vote Barry Obama
They are the stupidest of all!

B.O.

From Snow White and the Seven Dwarfs,
"Heigh Ho!" by Churchill & Morey

He digs digs digs digs digs digs digs with
a mind that don't think through
To dig dig dig dig dig dig dig's what Barry likes to do
It ain't no trick to get your vote
All he needs to say is Audacity of Hope
It is Mine! It is Mine! [It is mine! It is mine!]
Can you see the stars align?

He digs digs digs digs digs digs digs from early morn til night
He digs digs digs digs digs digs digs up every guilt from whites
He digs up delegates by the score
With a thousand voters, sometimes more
But we don't know what they dig him for
They'll make us all guinea pigs

[music interlude/ steam whistle]

B OH!
B OH!
B OH![B O!]
B OH!

[Chorus]

B O, B O
Off to DC he goes
[whistle]
B O,
B O, B O, B O
B O
The Emperor has no clothes
[whistle]

B O, B O

[*Whistle*]

Why Oh? B O
You know B O?
Do you want that
B O Hummmmm?
[*Chorus three times*]
[*fades out*]

Barry Obama (Mr. Bojangles)
Nitty Gritty Dirt Band: "Mr. Bojangles" by Bob Dylan

I knew a man Obama and he'd dance for you
With worn out views
No silver hair, a tidy shirt, and empty suit
He's just a fool
He jumped so high, jumped so high
Who is guiding this clown?

Schmit indicated FEMA's New Orleans
Was a litmus test
And how John McCain will give the eyes of age
And his way is best
But he's taking sides, sides we hate
He clicked his heels and stepped left.

You know the name Ms Clinton and she takes her licks
Across the chops
Obama? Seems like the MSM always takes his side
Gets more photo ops
He let go his church, let go his church
And now he is White House bound.

Barry Obama, Barry Obama
Barry Obama, Change!

His campaign is a minstrel show at those county fairs
Throughout the land
He speaks a treat how his Senate seat of two short years
Made him the man.
He promises hope, but what is hope?
After four short years will we grieve?

He says he's sure now his hands are pure for Honky's votes
He Hopes for Change
But most the time he drops a dime on his friends and foes

And those down-range
I shake my head, and as I shake my head
I hear myself ask Please!?

Please!!!!
Bury Obama, Bury Obama
Bury Obama's Chance

Run Run Run
Beach Boys "Fun Fun Fun" by Caleigh Peters

Well they got Obama's fans
And they cruised through the delegates, and how!
Seems they forgot all about those two Clintons
And the Re-pub's old man now
And from more Trinity smashing
Goes running just as fast as he can now

And we'll have fun fun fun til Obama takes our freedoms away
(fun fun fun til Obama takes our freedoms away)

Well the Right can't stand him
'cause he walks, talks and panders to race now
(he panders to race now, he panders to race)
His wife makes Mrs. Clinton look like a gal
that's loaded with grace now
(she's loaded with grace now, she's loaded with grace)
Those other guys couldn't catch her
But she's leading her own wild goose chase now
And we'll have fun, fun, fun til Obama takes our freedoms away.

Well you knew all along
Soros might be pushing for Obama
(Soros is right behind, waiting behind)
And since we lost a chance at Keyes
We've been thinking that Conserve's are all through now
(We wish we had Keyes, don't you wish we had Keyes?)
But you can come along with me
Cause there's nothing left for us to do now
And we'll just run run run when Obama takes our freedoms away.
(Repeat and fade)

Mr. Sandman
'Mr Sandman' made famous by the Andrews Sisters, parody inspired by Denny at Townhall.

Mr. Sandman gives us a dream
Ain't he the slickest that you've ever seen?
Give him big ears like little old Dumbo
He's just the cutest boy since li'l Black Sambo

Sandman, everyone sleeps
Why won't they wake up today, right now, please!
He just plants those magic beans
B. Obama makes them all scream

Mr. Sandman, Gives us a dream
But is that magic as good as it seems?
When off the cuff, just watch as he flounders
With ehm and ah and um, he's a dumbfounder

Sandman, Nobody sleeps
Can't we just shake them awake right now, Please?
But he just smiles, more tales he weaves
B. Obama's fairytale dreams!

Mr. Sandman, promises hope
But ain't he counting on us to be dopes?
With scripts he's great, this orator soaring
But we can't hear him cause the crowds are roaring

Sandman, Put it to rest
The MSM won't make you stand any test
Just keep it hushed and hide your agenda
Who cares if USA is 'bout to end-a

Mr. Sandman, terror we dread
Can we believe you won't offer our heads
But nightmares are a dream extreme
Will you kill the American dream?

Talking 'bout Obama's Blunderland
*Thanks for inspiration from Royce & Rolls,
here is "Winter Wonderland" by Felix Bernard*

Reverend King, Are you listenin'
Barry O's teeth are glistenin'
A miserable Right
Is not happy tonight
Contemplating Barry's Blunderland

Gone away, are the Clintons
Who'd a thunk that we'd miss 'em?
B.O. went along
With Reverend Wrong
Talk about Obama's Blunderland

None of Barry's Voters see the Strawman
But to all the rest he has no Brain
He says: Don't you trust me?
We say: No man!
Why would we want a Carter once again?

Later on, after chillin'
Wonderin' if he'll get a grillin'
The media swoons
They all sing his tune
Signin' on Obama's Blunderland

None of Barry's Voters see the Strawman
But we all wish he would seek a Brain
The Wizard found a brain in Mr. Strawman
But Barry's empty head will bring us pain

When he speaks, ain't he thrilling?
'specially when Kool-Aid swilling!
We wait for the gaffe, and wish we could laugh
Talkin' 'bout Obama's Blunderland

Change for Fools
Aretha Franklin's hit song "Chain of Fools"

Change, Change, Change, Change, Change, Change
Change, Change, Change, Change for fools
For Four Long years, Obama ran his campaign
But without a doubt his view was always long-range
He's got us where he wants us
We ain't nothin' but his tools
But what does it mean? If we allow him to rule?
Change, change, change,
Change for fools.

Every Change is not what you think
I might just supply that old missing link

[*'Hoo Hoo' rythmically repeats in background*]

You told me to leave him alone
I'd rather say go on home
You are sure he'll win it easy
But change for change's sake is just wrong!
He'll only cause us pain, pain , pain
Pain, pain, pain,
Change, change, change,
Change for fools

One of these mornings we'll see this guy is a fake
But up until then, yeah, I'll make what noise I can make
Change, change change,
Change, change, change
Change, change, change,
Change's for fools

Who is that New Demagogue Obama?
Patti Page had a hit song with "How Much is the Doggie in the Window"

Who is that new demagogue Obama?
(*Arf! Arf!*)
The one from old Harvard not Yale
Who is that new demagogue Obama?
(*Arf! Arf!*)
I do hope his campaign's No Sale

He once took a trip to California
And spoke in old San Francisco
He said some Americans are bitter
With him we aren't simpatico

Who is that new demagogue Obama?
(*Arf! Arf!*)
The one from old Harvard not Yale
Who is that new demagogue Obama?
(*Arf! Arf!*)
I do hope his campaign's No Sale

I read in the papers 'bout his Reverends
And others like Rezko and Ayers
If these are the fellows he hangs out with
I think we should all say our prayers.

I don't want more taxes or more spending
I don't want to fund the U.N.
I don't want to leave Iraq in 'pending'
I don't want Obama, Amen!

Who is that new demagogue Obama?
(*Arf! Arf!*)
The one from old Harvard not Yale
Who is that new demagogue Obama?
(*Arf! Arf!*)
I do hope his campaign's No Sale

Obama (Elvira)
From "Elvira" by the Oak Ridge Boys

Obama, Obama
Their heart's desire's Obama

Words that sound like heaven, Hear that Barry Whine
That boy can sure enough make his little light shine
Chris gets a funny feelin', Barry has no spine
They all think that it's Obama time

They're singin'
Obama, Obama
Our heart's desire is Obama

Give it Up O-Bama O-Bama Mau Mau
Give it Up O-Bama O-Bama Mau Mau
Hide your silver away!

Tonight we're gonna see him at the Democrat Campaign
And he's gonna promise all the perks he can, yes he can!
They're gonna jump and holler
When he steals their last two dollars
We shoulda listened to his old preacher man

They're singin'
Obama, Obama
Our heart's desire's Obama

Give it Up O-bama O-Bama Mau Mau
Give it Up O-Bama O-Bama Mau Mau
Hide your silver away!

Obama, Obama
Now sings the choir for Obama
Give it Up...
(*repeat chorus & fade*)

His Name's Barack Obama
O'connor & Stanford "McNamara's Band"
made famous by Bing Crosby.
This is another favorite of mine, but it's an OLDIE! Enjoy!

His Name's Barack Obama, And they think he's something grand
Although he's but a freshman, he's a Black from Lincoln Land
He uses teleprompters and with them he sounds a treat
But when he stumbles off the cuff, he chews on his two feet

Oh he speaks of change, leaving from down-
range, and our nation he wants to tax
McCain he stumps the same old tune, while Barry crowds attracts
And then when he guarantees oodles of loot
for corrupt U.N. demands
A debit to America is The Obama Plan

Right now he is rehearsin' for a very tough campaign
A Liberal Celebration, all the loonies call for change
When he beat Mrs. Clinton it was such a sight to see
Says she, "I never thought they'd choose Obama over me"

Oh he speaks of change, leaving from down-
range, and our nation he wants to tax
McCain he stumps the same old tune, while Barry crowds attracts
And then when he guarantees oodles of loot
for corrupt U.N. demands
A debit to America is The Obama Plan

Oh, his name is Jeremiah and from Trinity he came
He rants and raves, Obama saves his church from further shame
Guilt Rezko's found, Weather Underground, shady liaisons abound
But all is well 'Audacity' is great to have around

Oh, he wants to save the planet, with Al Gore he wears the green
More cap and trade, like an arcade, another silly scheme

He says that our thermostat must be reduced,
just like a bureaucrat,
But, by Jiminy I don't want to be his proletariat!

Oh he speaks of change, leaving from down-
range, and our nation he wants to tax
McCain he stumps the same old tune, while Barry crowds attracts
And then when he guarantees oodles of loot
for corrupt U.N. demands
A debit to America is The Obama Plan

Flipper
From the TV show: Flipper, theme written by Vars and Dunham

Barry's a flipper, clipper, Man, he is fright'ning!
No one believes he's smarter than he?
And with Obama, pulling our nation asunder
Soon he will plunder-from you and me!

Everyone loves that guy that we see
Ever so blind and gullible we
Flips he will do whenever we're near
But who will laugh come next year?

Barry's a flipper, clipper, Man, he is fright'ning!
No one believes he's smarter than he?
And with Obama, aiming our taxes to plunder
Soon we'll go under, asunder we'll be.

On the Road with Obama
Three Dog Night's "Road to Shambala" by D. Moore

Watch a day of troubles, Watch the way of pain
With that Saint Oh-bah-ma
Watch a day of sorrow, Just embrace the name
It's a shame, Oh-bah-ma.

(Chorus)
Ah Ooooh, yeah
Yeah, yeah, yeah, yeah, yeah *(X2)*
Everyone is Hopeful, everyone is Blind
On the Road with Obama
Everything is not ducky, Socialism we'll find
On that road with Obama.

(Repeat Chorus)

Why should we make time for the likes of Obama?
Why should we make time for the likes of Obama?

I will tell you sister he has power in his eyes
Hear the Lies from Obama
I will tell you brother he's a devil in disguise
Don't you vote for Obama

(Repeat Chorus)

Why should we be blind to the likes of Obama?
Why should we be blind to the likes of Obama?
Why should we be blind to the likes of Obama?
(repeat chorus and reprise and fade)

Ballad of Barack Obama
*From the TV show the Beverly Hillbillies.
Original theme by Paul Henning*

Come and listen to Obama and the words he said
A poor candidate,
Hardly known to use his head
Then one day he was chewin on his shoe
Said, "Darn that Al Gore, we can't drill for more crude."

Here, that is, ANWR, Coastal Sea.

Well the first thing you know Obama's in a fix
Liberals say 'The Repubs use dirty tricks'
Said "Californy proved he's no American'
Cause he don't cling to God and doesn't like guns.

Guns, that is, Second Amendment, Rights, indeed!

Well now it's time to say good bye to that Obama plan
But all of us will give our thanks for kickin' Clinton's can
If only we could find a better candidate than John
This whole election season would not be so awfully wrong.

He's silly, that is! Can he spell? Take the gloves off!

Y'all vote Right now, y'hear?

Go Home! B. Obama!
Lynyrd Skynyrd: 'Sweet Home Alabama"

Lib wheels keep on turning
Barry, he drones on listen in!
Reverend Wright can doubt our great land
I hear Obama once again
And I think it's a sin, yes.

Well I heard Mr Ayers was a mentor
Well, I heard Rezko was around
Well, I hope Real Sons will remember
Americans don't need them around, anyhow

Go Home B. Obama!
Most your lies are Blue
Go Home B. Obama!
Lord, I cannot vote for you.

In New Orleans they love their governor
Now Bush did all that he could do
Now FEMA-gate does not bother me
Don't your conscience bother you?
Tell the truth!

Go Home B. Obama!
Most your lies are Blue
Go Home B. Obama!
Lord, I cannot vote for you

Now Republicans aren't happy campers
And they've been known to pick a rube or two
Lord they piss me off so much
They kick me down when they're reeling Blue
Now how about you?

Go Home B. Obama!
Most your lies are Blue
Go Home B. Obama!
Lord, I cannot vote for you

Go Home B. Obama
(Go home Barry)
Most your lies are Blue
(and you know that is true)
Go Home B. Obama
(Lordy)
Lord, I cannot vote for you
[Yeah, B. Obama's not the answer.]

Lip Flapping Away!
From Paul Simon's "Slip Sliding Away"

(*Chorus*)
Lip Flapping away, Lip Flapping away
You know the nearer to their election,
The more they're lip flapping away.

Woah, I know a man,
He came from old Chi-town.
He looks so dashing and the voters wept to hear his sound
He has a chorus, And they all cheer
Their love for him is just so empowering,
I'm afraid to see the vote this year.

(*Chorus*)

I know a woman (who)
Became his wife
And then I hear the words she uses to describe her life
She says our nation ne'er made her proud
But if we criticize her rhetoric
Then Barack, himself, will scold the crowd.

(*Chorus*)

And don't you bother with Reverend Wrong
Although for twenty years Obama sang the same old song
He's come a long way voters to gain
Embraced his mentor and his grandma
Then he turned around and threw them from the train.

(*Chorus*)

Woah God only knows,
What are his plans?
That information's unavailable to the voting man

We're workin our jobs,
He'll collect our pay
Believe he's hoping for a new day when
in fact we can see it fade away

Lip Flapping away, Lip Flapping away
You know the nearer to their election,
The more they're lip flapping away.
(*Repeat & fade*)

Hello Barry!
*'Hello Dolly:' See Louis Armstrong, Movie Soundtrack
etc. Someone called Obama the Dali-Bama in
the comments. It inspired the following.*

Barry: Hello, Voters! Well, Hello Hopers
It's so nice to be in front where I belong
You're looking swell, Mama
Vote for O-Bama
I'm still runnin', John out-gunnin',
Although 'guns are wrong'
I feel like I'm swayin'
Those who are prayin'
I'm not just like Reverend Wright from old Chi-town
So, Bridge that gap, Voters
Fall right into my trap, Voters
Michelle's already picked her new ball gown!

Voters: Hello, Barry! Well Hello, Barry
It's a vice to be so glad you came along
You're leaning Left, Barry
You're so Deft, Barry
You're still runnin' Clintons stunnin'
But, No, guns aren't wrong.

You get the room swayin'
But we're all prayin'
You don't feel the same as that old Reverend Wrong..So...

Barry: Here's my point, Voters
Just smoke another joint, Voters

Voters: Promise you'll never smoke that way again!

Barry: I went away from the blight of that Lib-speak
The absentee voters to daze
But soon as I'm ushered into that White House Street
I'll then reconnoiter to my good old ways

Voters: What Good Old Days?

Barry: I tell you it's sweet!

Voters: Hello, well, hell no! Barry
Well hello, hey, look! He's scary!

Barry: Don't believe that stuff, I'm not an idle man!

Voters: What Idol, Man?

Barry: You're lookin' fat, Stanley
You'll lose some weight if you want to be manly.
We're all Overweight, and Underpaid and I've a plan!

Voters: I hear my teeth chatter

Barry: Do you hear your teeth chatter?

Voters: Our Founders' words matter!

Barry: Constitution in tatters?

Voters: And he's still advancing
helped by MSM So....

Barry: Golly, gee, voters
You've naught to fear from me voters!
That Constitution's just too old, my friends!

Voters: Tell us it's really not that Way!
We don't believe a word you say!

Barry and Voters:
Barry believes the means achieve the ends!

He Says He is for Changin'
Here's a Remix for Obama. "The Times They Are A-Changin' "- Billy Joel

Come gather 'round people
Where e'er you call home
And you'll see what the voters
Around you have known
It don't matter Obama
Has sins to atone
If the state to you is worth savin'
Then you'd better start voting
So he'll sink like a stone
For he says he is for changin'

Come voters and critics
All you women and men
Just keep your eyes wide
The chance won't come again
'Cause MSM sells you
Their own brand of spin
There's no tellin' who's in there gamin'
For we're losers now
If Obama wins
For he says he is for changin'

Come Senators, Congressmen
Please heed our call
You can't do things your way
You're the voice of us all
Our nation will need
A strong voice in the fall
There's a battle outside and it's ragin'
It is here on our borders
And we want the wall
For incumbents? They need a changin'!

Come mothers and fathers
Throughout the land
You must realize
That we need a strong hand
Our sons and our daughters
Inherit this land
Our country we must engage in
We need some maturity
At the command
Not some guy whose diapers need changin'

The time it is here
Your vote you must cast
Uphold our Republic
Let Liberty last
Don't let our freedoms
Fall into the past
Our nation is rapidly fadin'
Stop him before
The blue dye is cast
'Cause we don't need what he's changin'

I'm Ringin' in the Change
From 'Singin' in the Rain'
(As sung by Barack Hussein Obama)

I'm Ringin' in more Change
Just Ringin' in more Change
What a globalist feeling
I'm crafty my friend
I'm lappin' up dough
From folks just like Joe
The Guns will be next
And I'm ready to go

Let Pelosi and Reid
Help accomplish the deed
Go on, kill free speech
I cannot over-reach

I'm Barry Hussein
With a Brand-new domain
I'm Ringin' just ringin' in the Change

I'm drinkin' more Champagne
Your taxes down the drain
Old Wall Street is reeling
I'm Dopey McChange
I'll talk down my nose
BO smells like a rose
I'm ringin' just ringin' in the Change

Now it's a Recession!

Stevie Wonder is heavy into the Obama mania machine. I had to do this parody of his great hit: 'Superstition.' Enjoy.

(*Cue drums and funky music*)
Now it's a Recession! This guy's off the wall
Says it's a Depression! Stimulus for all
Trillion Dollar Bail- out!, broke the middle class
Sixty years of Bad Debt, the good things all are past
When you believed in Hope, what you don't understand
We all suffer,
Obamanation ain't the Way.
Isn't he audacious? Watch his bait and switch
Don't you see the problem? Bail- outs are a bitch,
This is like a bad dream, What he does is wrong
He don't wanna save us, but, we must stand strong.

When you believed B.O., what you don't understand
Is we'll suffer,
Obamanation ain't the Way. yeh yeh
Barry's Great Depression, nothin more to say
Liberty's Regression, Devil's here to stay
Trillion Dollar Bail-out! Broke the middle class!
Sixty years of Bad Debt, Good things all are past!

When you believed those things, and gave him command
Now we'll suffer
Obamanation ain't the Way, no, no, no

I'll Follow the One
Paul McCartney (The Beatles)
"I'll follow the Sun"

One day
You'll look
And see he's wrong
But tomorrow's a game
So you'll follow the One

Some day
You'll know
He took our guns
But tomorrow brings pain
'cause you followed the One

And now the time has come
Hawk or Dove,
He must Go
Although you hoped for change
He's deranged
And you know, oh

One day
You'll find
That he was wrong
And tomorrow brings pain
'Cause you followed the One

When Obama brings pain
You'll wish for your gun.

And soon the time will come
Hawk or Dove
He must go
And though he promised hope
Rope a Dope is B.O.

Oh. Oh. Oh.
Some Day
You'll see
That he was wrong
When tomorrow brings Pain
'Cause you followed the One

Blunder on Blunder

What constitutes a miracle, and what are lies, misdirection and deception? When the pilot averted death or disaster by landing his broken plane in the Hudson River, that was a miracle. Obama claims ethics, yet the choices for his administration are anything but ethical. Obama claims transparency, but his promise of that has not been demonstrated either. To have a politician actually hold themselves accountable for campaign promises might also be a miracle.

'Miracle of Miracles' from Fiddler on the Roof
original: Jerry Bock and Sheldon Harnick

Blunder on Blunder, Miracle of Miracles-
Dodge one for Barry once again,
Stood up for ethics - miracle of miracles-
Tax cheats enter Barry's den.
Blunder on Blunder, miracle of miracles-
We were afraid he was a clown
But as we knew so long ago, in Chicago
B.O. would make Bozo frown.

When B.O. forgave Geithner's 'err',
That was a miracle.
When Hillary got a Secretary Chair,
That was a miracle too!
But of all his miracles large and small
The most miraculous one of all
Is out of that worthless 'Hope and Change'
Now we see he is deranged!

Blunder on Blunder, miracle of miracles-
BO is POTUS of our land
Now that he's there no miracles or miracle -
Just more danger from his hand!

When US Air lost its engines, (guess!)
Was that a miracle?
But the pilot set it down in the Hudson (yes!)

That was a miracle true!
But if we want miracles large or small
To look to Barry's a silly call
For you see what's obvious to me
Miracles Won't come from he.

My Kind of Clown!
'My Kind of Town' (Chicago Is) Sinatra
(Van Heusen & Sammy Cahn)

Now this could only happen in the U.S.A.
And only happen in a town like this
So may I say to Liberals in love today
As you sing this song in a state of bliss...

He is My Kind of Clown, Obama Is
My kind of Clown, Obama Is
The One, Bi-racial brew
And MSM smiles at you
And each time I roam, Obama is
TXTing my phone, Obama is
Why I just grin like a gnome
He's my kind of clown.

My kind of clown, Obama is
My kind of clown, Obama is
So full of Razzmatazz
Hope and Change, all that Jazz
And each time I think, Obama is
My KoolAid drink, Obama is
My EO Token, Obama is
The One from Oprah, Obama is
One clown that won't make us frown
He's my kind of Clown.

How Do You Solve a Problem Like Obama?
To the tune of "How do you solve a problem like Maria" from Sound of Music. This song just seems to lend itself to parody, you will see it again!

Chant:
They think that Barry O's
A Messiah now, and so
No one dares to challenge his first week as crap!
After booing Dubya's speech
Being friends is out of reach
But we lack the votes to make them shut their trap!
We've even heard he's planning to close GITMO.

And though Barry said 'Unite'
We'll not yield without a fight
It's not racist, we just don't agree with him!
Obama Nation: What a Moil
They expect to reap our toil
Pushing bail-outs, and more taxes, wallets thin!

But....I'd like to say a word in his behalf
Obama Makes Me LAUGH!

(cue music)
How do you solve a problem like Obama
How do you counter all this talk of "Hope"
How do you solve a problem like Obama
A novice at best, a puppet we think, a Dope!
Many a man has tried to be the POTUS
Even some women too, but that's a joke
The last man we had to choose
Is famous for dodging shoes
And now all we have is talk of change and hope.
Oh, How do you solve a problem like Obama?
How can we stop him with his racist style?

How do you solve a problem like Obama?
How many scandals has he had so far?
How do you solve a problem like Obama?
He seems so immune to reason, this idol star
Many the times he's stumbled or mis-spoken
Many the times he's had reporters swoon
But why should he get a pass
His house too is made of glass
Why should we all just dance for this buffoon?
Oh How do you solve a problem like Obama?
We must oppose him, 'til his time is past.

You Love Me 'cause I ROCK!
A parody of 'She Loves Me Like a Rock' by Paul Simon, as sung by Barack Obama.

When I was a little boy, (but don't you call me: boy)
I had some trouble with all my names (when I was just a boy)
I'd say now who do?
Who Do you think I'm fooling? (when I was just a boy)
I'll be a coronated boy (and won't it bring me joy)
Call me PEBO and on Tuesday 'Sire'
Oh, Obama loves, I love me
They'll get down on their knees and hug me
Like they love me for Iraq
They'll rock me though I mock the sages
They love me.
They love me, love me, love me, love me

Now that I'm grown to be a man (grown to be a man)
And now P-BO will be my name (grown to be a man)
I'll say now who do?
Who do you think I'm fooling? (grown to be a man)
I'm an idoliz'in man (grown to be a man)
I can snatch a little history
I'm Obama love me, please love me
Just get down on your knees and hug me
You'll love me cause I Rock!
I'll rock you like the 'Rock of Ages'
You'll love me
You'll love me, love me, love me, love me!

And now that I'm President (now the president)
No need for Congress to call my name (I'm the President!)
I'll Say now, who do?
Who do you think you're fooling? (who
do you think you're fooling)
I've got the Presidential seal (I'm the President!)
I'm up on that Presidential Podium!

Obama loves me
You'll love me
You'll get down on your knees and hug me
You'll love me cause I ROCK!
I'll rock you like the 'Rock of Ages'
You'll love me

Fade Out:
You'll love me, love me, love me, love me
(You'll love me cause I rock!)

They Call His Name Obama
From Paint Your Wagon 'They Call the Wind Maria'

Obama Obama
They call his name: Obama
Obama's got a middle name
Hussein's his amplifier
Hussein may just inspire fear
And they call on him: Obama

Obama throws his weight around
And runs from Blago's lyin'
Obama shakes Chicago's hounds
Above the fray he's flyin'
Obama Obama
They call his name: Obama

Before we knew Obama's name
A gal both pale and shinin'
Thought she'd be next, And not Hussein
But the One caused her sidelinin'

But then one day they left that girl
They left her far behind him
And now we're lost, so doggone lost
No Clinton can outshine him
Obama Obama
They call his name Obama

When he was just a candidate
No name would work for Barry
To say Hussein somehow was wrong
Didn't want the fate of Kerry

And now we have this President
And no one seems to worry
That Muslim roots might represent

A need to-be from Missouri
Obama Obama
They call his name Obama
Obama Obama!
Or Hussein, is he.

Mr. Cellophane!
Dedicated to the man who wants to be transparent!
From the Broadway show and movie Chicago:
" Mr. Cellophane" by Ebb & Kander

Obama:
If someone stood up and said "change "
And raised his voice's decibel range
And waved his arm to thrill your leg
You'd notice him.

If someone from the movie shows
Yelled "Liar" to those who oppose
And said "Repubs have bubonic plague!"
You'd notice him.

And even without clucking like a hen
Those roosting chickens come back now and then
Unless, of course, that personage should be
Invincible, imperviable me!

Cellophane
Mister Cellophane
Shoulda been my name
Mister Cellophane
No matter who once knew me
Talk right by me!
I'm just a saint I swear!

I tell ya
Cellophane
Mister Cellophane
It's my other name
Mister Cellophane
Don't see no lies or scandal
It's my handle
I'm just a saint I swear!

Suppose a colleague was a rat
My bus soon will just run him flat
Rahm sends them fish and I'll say "I don't know"
Don't notice him!

Suppose you had a Senate seat
And Sixty is the magic number feat
Blagojevich is a man I never knew
Don't notice him!

A politician's mark is everywhere
Do as I say not as I do is fair
And nowhere is that adage more than true
Than when that human bein' next to you
Is equivocating, bloviating
You know who.....

Cellophane
Mister Cellophane
It's my claim to fame
Mister Cellophane
Don't see no lies or scandal
That's my handle
I'm just a saint I swear!

I tell ya
Cellophane
That's my claim to fame
Mister Cellophane
Cause I say I'm transparent
It's apparent
There's not a scandal there
There's never any scandal there!

Chapter Five:
2008 Election and New Administration

Raise Your Hand for the Man with the Plan

Lynn Anderson wrote a great song called "Put Your Hand in the Hand of the Man from Galilee" It seems so appropriate to the Left's new messiah, so here's a remix. If he continues to implode, it looks likely that it will be easier for McCain to defeat him than if Hillary was the opposition (Hence the first verse). Obama has plans to change America. I don't like his plans. I don't want higher taxes, global warming influencing our energy needs, nor do I wish to pander to terrorists and diminish our national defense. He is not the messiah. He is a dangerous man for our nation. He will make Carter look like a great statesman. [12 August 2008 blog entry]

Raise your hand for the man with the plan that's still like Carter's
Raise your hand for the man with the plan to save the seas
Take a look for yourself and you will see he likes that royal 'we'
So raise your hand for the man with the plan, not Hillary.

Everytime I look to see that Demo crook I start to tremble
When I listen to him speak then I freak, "America's in peril!"
I'm not buyin' what he's sellin' 'cause there's no
way of tellin' if he's friend or Pharisee
And it causes me pain, you know I'm just one of the bourgeoisie

Abandon the man with the plan, it's a plan that's still like Carter's
Abandon the man with the plan, there's
no chance he'll part the seas
Take a look for yourself and you will see the danger I foresee,
By raisin' your hand for the man with the plan, Dem's nominee

'Bama wants us all to vote for some change
when we reach the election
Seems he wants to forget what they did on Nine-Eleven
Barry don't like Iraq don't support the attack,
but you do what you must do
He should be ashamed, don't you think
we ought to see it through?

Abandon the man with the plan, it's a plan that sounds like Carter
Abandon the man with the plan don't believe he can part the seas
Take a look at his plan to inflate your tires not drill for energy
Abandon the man with the plan don't elect their nominee
(*Repeat*)

He'll Spin it Easy
Ringo Starr "It Don't Come Easy"

He'll spin it easy, you know he'll spin it easy
He'll spin it easy, you know he'll spin it easy

Do what Barry says or he might not be the Prez
He can win the prize quite easy
Don't worry that he lies, he's about to win the prize
It's enough to make you queasy

Don't look into his past, no trouble borrow
He will take DC at last, Brave New World is our tomorrow

He don't ask for much, he just wants us to trust
He can fix health care quite easy
Don't worry about race, he's a bi-racial face
And on Terrorists he's easy

Don't worry that he'll add a little drama
He understands the game, don't you know he's the Obama?

Forget about the facts, he'll only raise your tax
Funding socialism's easy
He knows what he wants to do, it don't matter about you
He will pick our pockets easy

Imagine what he'll do with another hurricane
FEMA will be strong because Bush no longer is to blame

For Barry to relate he shuns a tough debate
And he's starting to move centrist
He'll get his votes from you, and all illegals too
Only later will he un-twist.

Worried that he'll pander to the UN?
Don't you know it's true that he'd rather impress CNN?

Do what Barry says or he might not be the Prez
He has MSM to tell you
He wants a social change, and to pull-out from down-range
It's enough to make you queasy.

He'll spin it easy, he says he'll win it easy...
We all feel queasy, you know we all feel queasy....

I've been a Maverick!
"My Way" (Sinatra) by Paul Anka, J. Revaux, C. Frankois
For the Election!

Wake up! The end is near
And for this race the falling curtain
My friends, Election's here
We need your vote, is that not certain?

I've lived a Long, Long time
I've weathered much, and I'm no peacenik
But more, much more than this
I've been a Maverick!

Regrets, I've had my share
But Sarah's here, I choose to mention
With her I'll bring reform
And not his 'change': NO 'Bama Nation

I'm G.O.P. perforce
Not really 'Right,' if you must nitpick
I'm more than the dark horse
I am the Maverick!

Yes, there are times, I cross the aisle
And SNL still makes me smile
Though Tina Fey plays Sarah dumb
Joe plumber knows BO's no 'One'
Sarah and me need victory!
We are both Mavericks!

I've run, campaigned and tried
But it's not me that's scared of losing
BO will us divide
And you won't find it so amusing

To think our nation's pick's
At voters' polls, not ACORN's sly tricks
Oh No, Joe Plumber knows
We are the Mavericks!

For what is the Right, what has it got?
I won't be soiled by what they've wrought
I'll say the things I truly feel
And will not ride on Bush's heels
This prisoner knows, I've took the blows
Vote For the Mavericks!

Blunderful Hopenchangin'

A great waltz from the old movie "Hans Christian Anderson" Here's my version of "Wonderful, Wonderful, Copenhagen" by Frank Loesser.

Blunderful, dunderful, Hopenchangin'
Obama's mantra we sound
'Neath his lantern bright
Shines a magic light
Let us think! He'll bring us down

To blunderful, dunderful, Hopenchangin'
But does he mean you and me?
Once he's there to stay
Will we rue the day?
Crying Hopenchangin',
We want some wonderful, Hopenchangin' from he!

I swear I'm not antiblack
But he's not a brainiac
Though he's artful, charm is his forte
And there they stand, Biden and he
With a message to charm and obey

Blunderful, dunderful, Hopenchangin'
[musical interlude as we picture Biden and Obama waltzing]
Blunderful, Dunderful, Hopenchangin'
Barry can only expound
See his resume
Nothing's there you say?
Let us think! This man's a clown!

For Blunderful, Dunderful, Hopenchangin'
Changin' the land of the free?
Once he's there to stay
Will we rue the day?
We bought Hopenchangin'
Blunderful, Dunderful, Hopenchangin' from he?

If I Were Obama
From Fiddler On the Roof "If I Were a Rich Man"
by Sheldon Harnick & Jerry Bock

If I were Obama,
Ya ha deedle deedle, bubba bubba deedle deedle dum.
All day long I'd prove that I was dumb
If I were Obama man!

I wouldn't have to try hard
Ya ha deedle deedle, bubba bubba deedle deedle dum.
I'd just let the MSM stand guard
And propose I am your Idol, man!

I'd tell them just to keep your car tires inflated
And dare them label me a clown
A simple task will save all our oil below

No need to drill, We'll save more oil with a tune up
Than if we'd drill more from our ground
So what, we're going nowhere, it's for show!

I'd have more friends like Wright and Rezko and Ayes and Dohrn
Don't believe what you might hear!
And each loud 'erh' and 'uhm' and 'tuh' and 'fer'
Would sound like a valley girl you fear
As if to say, "Who taught Obama, Man?"

If I were Obama
Ya ha deedle deedle, bubba bubba deedle deedle dum.
All day long I'd prove that I was dumb
If I were Obama man!
I wouldn't have to try hard
Ya ha deedle deedle, bubba bubba deedle deedle dum.
I'd just let the MSM stand guard
And propose I am your Idol, man!

I see my wife, my Michelle, looking like a rich man's wife
Oh boy don't she have thin-skin!
Lay off her or you'll have to deal with me

I see her standing with Ayers, Wright's strutting like a peacock
Oy, what a nasty mood they're in
Screaming at our country day and night.

The most important men around will come to fawn on me!
They should ask me to advise them
To prevent the world's demise...
"If you please, Barry Obama...'
Pardon me, Barry Obama.'
Posing problems that would cross a Magi's eyes!
OY OY OY OY OY OY!

And it won't make one bit of difference
if you think I'm right or wrong
Don't you think Messiah really knows?

If I were Prez, I'd have the time to unpack
And stop all the campaign stress and strife
And maybe point my rug to the Eastern wall

And I'd discuss my Marxist plans with my
Cabinet, maybe even every day.
Don't you see me now with my cabal?

If I were Obama
Ya ha deedle deedle, bubba bubba deedle deedle dum.
All day long I'll prove that I'm the One
If I were Obama man!

I wouldn't have to try hard
Ya ha deedle deedle, bubba bubba deedle deedle dum.
I'd just let the MSM stand guard
And propose I am your Idol, man!

Big Marshmallow!
Here is my version of Donovan's "Mellow Yellow"

I'm just mad at Obama
Obama's mad at McCain
But why be mad B. Obama?
Ads are part of the game
(Refrain)
You're just a big marshmallow
(Quite Right!)
Why should you be so yellow?
(Quite Right!)
Why should we trust this fellow?

Voters mad about Barry
Barry's madness I see
But, why be mad about Barry?
When he's just a Prez wannabe?

He's just a big marshmallow
(Quite Right)
He certainly is yellow
(Quite Right)
Why would we trust this fellow?

McCain served and he did fly
Was held in a torturer's cell
Served his country with honor
His courage don't need a hard sell

He's not a big marshmallow
(Too Right!)
He's certainly Not Yellow!
(Quite Right)
I'd rather trust this fellow!

Ba ba ba-de-dah Bah bah

Ba ba ba-de-dah Bah
Ba ba ba-de-dah Bah Bah
Ba ba ba-de-dah Bah!
Oh Barry's a marshmallow!
(That's right)
His spine is painted yellow!
(That's right)
Why would we trust this fellow?

Mr. Democrat
From Paul Simon's 'Mrs. Robinson"

And here's to you, Mr. Democrat
Barry loves you more than you will know
God blesses you, Mr. Democrat
Heaven sent that face and now you rave,
Hey hey hey

I'd like to know a little bit about him for my files
I'd think we all should learn to help ourselves
Look around you all you see are more pathetic lies
Polls abound they've found real voters stay at home

And here's to all you Republicans
Barry hides much more than you will know
wo wo wo
God bless you, please, Mr. 'Publican
Heaven holds this race and we must pray
Hey, Hey, hey, Hey Hey Pray!

Pride has got him hyping race where ever Barry goes
Sounds like Elmer Gantry, he's a cupcake
It's an open secret just like Reverend Wright and Ayers
Most of all he tries to hide from all he said

Koo Koo Ka Choo Mr. Democrat
Barry loves you, and you ought to know
wo wo wo
Our wealth he'll freeze, Mr. Democrat
Hope will never keep the wolf at bay
Hey Hey Hey

Sitting on a sofa some November afternoon
Did we hear the candidates debate?
Laugh about it, shout about it
When you've got to choose
Every way you look at it we lose

Where have you gone, Thomas Jefferson
Our nation needs our Constitution true!
Ooo ooo ooo
What's that you say, Mr.Democrat
Liberty has left and we must pay
Hey hey hey, Hey hey hey

Barack's Magic History Tour
Magical Mystery Tour (Lennon/McCartney)
It was inevitable.! I'd been wanting to use this song for a long time. After Barack's July 2008 junket (the self-proclaimed NON Campaign trip) where he instructs the world on history, wants to re-make history, indeed his trip was characterized by the media as 'history-making'... (gag!)

Barack! Barack's magic history tour!
Barack! Barack's magic history tour.
Barack! AND IT'S A REVELATION
Barack's magic history tour
Barack! HE REPRESENTS ALL NATIONS
Barack's magic history tour
The magical history tour is seeking to fake it today
Seeking the voters to sway.
Barack! Barack's magic history tour
Barack! Barack's magic history tour.
Barack! HE'S GOT EVERYTHING YOU NEED,
Barack's magic history tour.
Barack DISILLUSION GUARANTEED,
Barack's magic history tour.
Barack's magic history tour is hoping you voters to sway
Hoping to fake it today!

[spoken]
When a man takes a junket for a magical history tour,
you all know what to expect.
He guarantees us the gyp of a lifetime!
And that's just what we get!
An indelible magical history tour!

Barack! Barack's magic history tour
Barack! Barack's magic history tour.
Barack! AND IT'S A REVELATION
Barack's magic history tour
Barack! HE REPRESENTS ALL NATIONS

Barack's magic history tour
The magical history tour reveals Barry's nature today
See Megalomania pay!
Barack's magic history tour! White Coats should take him away
White Coats should take him away, That's what I say

You Know They'd Rather Deal With Me!
Based on the Turtles song "She'd Rather Be with Me"

Come World, Vote for Barry now
Commander of the waiting world is me!
'Cause my world, Needs no guns around
Because you know they'd rather deal with me!

Me oh my, magic guy is what I am
Tell you why? You understand?
As you sigh, say 'Yes, He Can!"

A. Q. and the Taliban
Prob'ly think that I'm the perfect choice
But A. Q. and the Taliban
Know with me they'll have a better voice!

Me oh my, magic guy is what I am
Tell you Why? You? Understand?
As you sigh, say, "Yes, He Can!"

Ba ba ba ba ba ba ba
Ba ba ba ba ba ba ba
Ba ba ba ba ba ba ba
Ba ba ba ba ba ba ba

Some Libs, think Obama's sound
Love to listen to the things he said
But my word! He isn't so profound
'Cause above the neck he is brain-dead!

Me oh my, magic guy? Oh NO my friend!
Tell you why? Please understand!
He'll just fake it til The End!

He thinks, others buy his hope
And he'll handle everything just fine

But I know, he's a scary dope
And you know he hasn't got one
You know you'd surely spot one
You know he hasn't got a spine!
Ba ba ba ba ba ba ba
You know he hasn't got a spine!
(repeat & fade)

ACORN

From Hans Christian Anderson. "Inchworm" by Frank Loesser

ACORN, ACORN
Altering what voter's told
You and your arithmetic
Stinks like an abattoir

(*Chorus*)

One and One are Four
Four and One are Eight
Eight and Two are Sixteen
Stealing more votes! ACORN's dirty too

Franken, Franken
Minnesota's loser boy
You and your arithmetic
Votes for you are bizarre

(*Chorus*)

Just like, Barry
He had ACORN on his side
They and their arithmetic
He'll probably be czar

ACORN, ACORN
Disenfranchised!
Voter Fraud
When will voters stop and see
How dangerous you are?

ACORN Keeps Fallin' on My Head
From Butch Cassidy and the Sundance Kid, "Raindrops Keep Fallin' on my Head." (Bachrach) You can guess the subject.

ACORN keeps fallin' on my head
I'm just like the guy who needs to pack the votes instead
You should have a fit
Those ACORNS keep fallin' on my head they keep fallin'

So what if that Michelle Malkin' took me on?
And she said she didn't like the way I got things done
Cheatin' for the job!
Those ACORNS keep fallin' on my head they keep fallin'

But there's one thing I know
The rules I bend completely won't defeat me
It won't be long till all my friends are back to greet me.

ACORN keeps fallin' on my head
And you don't believe your eyes that we'll be turnin' RED
Lyin's my disease
'Cause you're never gonna stop my reign by complainin'
Because I'm Me!
ACORN helps me you see?

[*trumpet*]

It won't be long till Ayers and Wright are back to greet me.

ACORN keeps falllin' on my head
But I'm not afraid because I have them all in bed
Lyin' just for me
'Cause you're never gonna stop my reign by complainin'
Because I'm Me!
Nothin's worrying me

I'm at GITMO Terror Bastion!

I'm sure you all heard the tale about the GITMO 'detainee' that was provided medical care and a state-of-the-art artificial limb (leg) that was later released to commit another terrorist attack. At least, I **hope** you heard about it, even though it was not widely publicized in the media.
Mick Jagger & Keith Richards' song; "I Can't Get no Satisfaction"

I'm at GITMO, Terror Bastion
Prefer GITMO to Legal Action
Libbies Lie, and they lie, and they lie, and they lie
I'm at GITMO, I'm at GITMO

When a land mine took my leg
In my latest terror action
At GITMO they replaced my peg
With a Sweet Brand New Contraption
And now I am back in action!
I love GITMO, and don't you know

That's What I say! Rip off the USA
I love GITMO Terror Bastion
Fresh from GITMO back in Action
'Cause I lie, and I lie, and I lie, and I lie
I love GITMO I love GITMO

When I'm prayin' to the east
And a guard hands me my luncheon
One of three square meals, at least
But the Libs think it's a dungeon
Where the USA's the beast
I love GITMO, oh yo yo yo

Hey hey hey, Rip off the USA
Life at GITMO's a distraction
ife at GITMO! Prepare for action

But I lie, and I lie, and I lie, and I lie
I love GITMO! oh yo yo yo

When I'm set loose again to hate
And I'm plottin' this and I'm shootin' that
And I think how I gained this weight
And I wish I could go back a maybe next week
'Cause those three squares and games were oh so sweet
And at least in there I could rest and sleep
I miss GITMO! oh Yo Yo Yo
Hey hey hey, That's what I say
I miss GITMO, I miss GITMO
I miss GITMO Terror Bastion
Terror Bastion! Terror Bastion! Terror Bastion!

He's Still Just B.O. To Me
From Billy Joel, "It's Still Rock and Roll to Me"

What's the matter with words I'm swearing?
Can't you tell that he's changed the tide?
Maybe I should try that KoolAid flavor
Welcome back to the great divide.
Where have you been hidin out lately, Reason?
We can't sit back and let the Libs get by with treason.
Everybody's talkin' bout the new Prez
Funny, but it's still just B.O. to me.

What's the matter with the car I'm driving?
Can't you tell that it guzzles gas?
Should I get a little hybrid number?
If I don't then I'll lose my ass.
Nowadays you must be environmental
A hybrid's gonna save the Earth! No Excremental!
Slam dunk, blows chunks, even if it all stunk
It's still just B.O. to me.

Oh, it doesn't matter what they say in the papers
Or the dribble in the magazines
There's a new man in town
And he'll just bring us down like a chad in a voting machine
Or maybe a mujahideen.

How about we share a few stemwinders?
'Cause the truth soon will be forbid.
We could really start a group of resistance
Just the way our forefathers did.
Don't waste your money on a Wall Street planner
401Ks are the new Katz and Jammer
Next raise, new days, tax craze, anyways
It's still just B.O. to me.

What's the matter with the G.O. P.ers?
Don't you know that they're out of luck?
Should I try to be a gracious loser?
If you are, then you're just a schmuck!
Don't you know about the new Hope and Changen?
B.O.'s plans will be so big and far-rangin'!
It's the new deal, new seal, done deal, and I feel
It's still just B.O. to me!

Everybody's talkin' bout the new man
Funny, but it's still just B.O. to me.

Peggy the Moocher
From inspiration supplied by Michelle Malkin's column about Peggy the Moocher. Here is my remix of Cab Calloway's famous song 'Minnie the Moocher.'

Folks, now here's a story about Peggy the Moocher
Some think she's just a bag o' douch-er
She drank the love-fest Koolaid grail
Cause Barry has a heart as big as a whale

Hodey-ho-dee-hodey-ho
Hidey-hi-dee-hidey-hi
Heedey-hee-dee-heedey hee
Hodey-ho-dee-hodey-ho

Now she caught the smoke from a bloke named Barry
She loved him though he was scary
He came to fame from Chicago-town
And now she thinks he should be wearing a crown

Hodey-ho-dee-hodey-ho
Hidey-hi-dee-hidey-hi
Heedey-hee-dee-heedey hee
Hodey-ho-dee-hodey-ho

Now she had a dream, old Barry streamin'
He promised things that she was needin'
He'll give her a home that is paid with tax he steals
Now she expects gas to propel her wheels

Hodey-ho-dee-hodey-ho
Hidey-hi-dee-hidey-hi
Heedey-hee-dee-heedey hee
Hodey-ho-dee-hodey-ho

Now he can give her a new house from other sources
Each meal she eats Obama sends, of courses

He'll spread around the wealth in millions of dimes
So Mary never has to work through any hard times

Hodey-ho-dee-hodey-ho
Hidey-hi-dee-hidey-hi
Heedey-hee-dee-heedey hee
Hodey-ho-dee-hodey-ho

Poor Men, Poor Men, Poor Men

Can't Help Feelin' It's Rigged this Time

From the musical Showboat. "Can't Help Lovin' Dat Man Of Mine" by Kern & Hammerstein. (Just in case anyone is in the dark about how in the tank the Main stream media (MSM) was for Obama during the election.)

(MSM sings)
"Wish it was him, We've gotta lie
Obama has to be the new guy"
Can't help feelin' it's rigged this time

Tell me he's magic, tell me he's owed
Tell me it's tragic, maybe it's so
Can't help feelin' it's rigged this time

When he takes the stage, all the voters rage
But when he steps down we see his lies
The newsmen cry

He can explain his taxes are free
Tax breaks for him means no cash for me
Can't help doubtin' that man this time

When we vote today, Will our voice hold sway?
When those ACORN voters stand in line?
Lipstick's on swine

Fish gotta swim, Libs gotta lie
MSM's in the tank for this guy
Can't help feelin' it's rigged this time.

His Sleaze, Hacks and Thieves
From Cher's hit song: 'Gypsies, Tramps and Thieves.'
Inspired by the Hackers of Palin's e-mail.

Palin's one on a ticket that Conservatives know
Obama-bots advance and the mud-slinging flows
Soros would do whatever he could
Breach e-mail at Yahoo, tell a couple whoppers to stop her good

Chorus: More sleaze, hacks and thieves
We hear lies from the people for this clown
I call them
His Sleaze, Hacks and Thieves
But very soon the Right will come around
And bring Obama down

Dems love this boy, he's just a schlemiel
Fills 'em with pride, thinks he'll be the New Deal
He is so Green, He is "sent"; the 'One!"
Loads us up with Bull-schist!
Obama had his shot and soon we'll see him undone.

(*Chorus*)

I know who he's foolin' 'Cause they taught him well
With his smooth Chicago style
Three months later he's a man in trouble
And we won't see him in a while! Uh-huh
We won't see him in a while, uh-huh

We'll sink his battlewagon, no more travelin' show
Obama won't advance from the money they throw
Patriots do whatever they should
We won't read his e-mail,
Won't need to tell whoppers,
We'll just flip him the bird.

(*Chorus repeats and fades*)

We Need a Little Litmus!

For those who think that the court cases to ask Obama for a certificate of live birth to verify his eligibility to be our POTUS is a right-wing-nut conspiracy, I say: If it's no big deal, then release the information and move on, Obama. Otherwise, provide the documents! Why do you have three entire Law Firms committed to combating these suits? Be Transparent!

So, from MAME: "We Need a Little Christmas" by Jerry Herman

Why is it Folly?
To ask Obama for his Birth Certificate?
It might be shocking
To find we've chosen someone who is not legit now!
For we need a little Litmus
Right this very minute
Give it to the SCOTUS
MSM will spin it
And we need a little Litmus
Right this very minute
It hasn't hung a single jury
But, Barry, Dear, we're in a hurry
So, Climb off your High Horse
Provide a document that satisfies our law
If I'm a fruitcake
I will not mind as long as you have gravitas now
For I've grown a little doubtful
Grown a little Sadder
Grown a little Older
But this makes me madder
And we need a little shaker
Underneath his ladder
We need a little Litmus now.

Haul out Alinsky
Bring out the longest string of lies I've ever seen
And look at Blago
It seems Obama wants to move away from him now

For we need a little Litmus
Right this very minute
When and what did he know
Don't you see he'll spin it?
And we need a little Litmus
Right this very minute
It hasn't hung a single jury
But, Barry, Dear, we're in a hurry
So Climb off your High Horse
Provide an explanation that is credible
If I'm a fruitcake
I will not mind as long as you have gravitas now
For we need a little Litmus
Need a little candor
Need a little honest
Man, that's what we're after
And we need a little sunshine
On this presidential crafter
We need a little Litmus Now!

Oklobama!

Inspired by David Letterman: From the "Top Ten Signs Barack Obama is Overconfident: Proposed bill to change Oklahoma to 'Oklobama'"
So here it is! From the Musical Oklahoma (Rodgers & Hammerstein)

There ain't no better time to learn to think
But you must listen to what all he says
You might miss it if you start to blink
Thinking 'bout Obama as the brand new Prez
Brand new Prez?
That's what he says
Gonna buy you all a little more taxation
Health care for your neighbor, ain't it aggravatin'
Says he'll go on Oprah, where they're bound to swoon
Plenty of air! The new 'oil' boon
Plenty of words, and it's a joke
Plenty of Change and Plenty of Hope
OOOOOOOk-lobama,
Where the wind he blows is seeking Change
And the waving seas, will soon recede,
As he conquers climate, sun and rain!
OOOOOOOk-lobama,
Every night his hunny-lamb will sigh
Don't you know I'm proud, I'll say it loud
When the White House welcomes you and I!
We know he belongs to the Left (yo ho)
And the Left will just leave us bereft!
And when he says
Yeeow! *Uhhh* Yip Aye Yo *Uh* yay!
He's only sayin'
I'm doin' fine, I'm Obama!
Oklobama! OK!
Repeat All
Okla-okla-Okla-Okla-Okla-Okla
Okla-okla-Okla-Okla-Okla-Okla...
We know he belongs to the Left (yo ho)
And the Left will just leave us bereft!

And when he says
Yeeow! *Errr* Yip Aye Yo *Uh* yay!
He's only sayin'
I'm doin' fine, I'm Obama!
Oklobama!
O-K-L-O-B-A-M-A Oklobama! Yeow!

Teleprompter Song

Why does a press go along with a scripted news conference? The Teleprompter has become a running gag with this president. Unfortunately, the joke is on us.
'Wichita Lineman' by Glenn Campbell

I am Obama's Teleprompter
Give him lies by trainload
Hookin' up the One with another smelly load

You'll see he never does perspire
Prepared answers rule the day
And this great Teleprompter
Tells him what he has to say!

I know I can't go on vacation
'Cause he can't speak off-hand
And don't you know that wretched mouth
Is reigning over our land?

And he feeds you what he wants to
And he wants to change our land
And this great Teleprompter
Is here to give him a hand!

Hail to the Chief
Original words by Albert Gamse Music by James Sanderson
Mrs. Paddy's Version:

Hail to the Chief, It's Obama's Teleprompter
Hail to the Chief! Don't be frightened by the fall
Hail to the Chief! We are now Obamanation
Soon we will fail due to his global gall!

No more will we strive to make our country grander
Our just rewards can be confiscated now!
When did we choose to adopt this Marxist traitor?
Who can we turn to? To Hell with the Chief!

Dodd and Pelosi and Reid all join his army
Geithner and all engineered our sure demise
Tyranny, taxes and lisping scolds from Barney
Selling the snake oil that they are so wise.

Hail to the Chief, honor B.O.'s Teleprompter
Without his help no news conference is held
Newsmen and women all bow to Barry's wishes
So much for Freedom of Press, it's gone to hell.

Ballad of B.O.
From the Beverly Hillbillies theme song by Paul Henning.

Come and listen to my story 'bout that guy B.O.
Some call him JugEars, Others use the term: Dumbo
Don't care what you call him, 'cause to me it's plain to see
That the guy and his friends want to kill our Liberty!

Amendment Two! Guns Indeed!

Well the first thing he did clued us to where he stands
A 'scoop' for the Arabs then Closing GITMO planned
Said Bush Secret papers would be free for all to see
But BO's proof of birth is behind lock and key.

School Records too, but he's no liar!

Well, now it's time to say goodbye to BO and his ilk
We know that he can't turn those pork-ears into something silk
You're invited to the White House, th' Wagyu beef is grand!
To have a farewell party for what made this Freedom's Land!

So much for ethics! It's time for TEA!
Y'all think about it now!
Y'Hear?

Faces

Thanks to the poster known as Tea Party for the inspiration. Tea Party wrote the following on a Michelle Malkin column. "You have a way with words. Fauxtographs. Just the word for the fauxAmerican, fauxchristian, fauxsenator, fauxleader, fauxflagwaver, fauxpatriot, the one the only fauxbama."

I think this is great fodder for future parodies! THANKS to Michelle and Tea Party! This needs to be a little up-beat from the original song. From "Traces" by Buddy Buie / James Cobb / Emory Gordy

Taking fauxtographs,
Family shots with wife and daughters
Campaign hype and flash,
Michelle talks with Barbara Walters
Faces to love, Don't ya know?
But it won't work out right
Faces to love

Hype beyond compare,
Magazines with glossy covers,
Empty suits he wears,
Hardbound books with slick dustcovers
Faces to love, don't ya know?
But it won't work out right
Faces to love

Just close your eyes
And say a prayer
That we will see beyond
Those fauxtographs that glare
Out there, oohhh

Traces of hope for the right
That we'll come back and show
Those faces are faux!
Lies and Hype!
Ohh oh oh ohhhh

There Are No Strings on Me!
Obama, Naive? Megalomaniac? or Puppet? From Pinocchio: "There are No Strings on Me." Original by Leigh Harline, Ned Washington

OBAMA:
I've got no strings
That make me dance
To feed me lines, Give me a Chance
If I had strings
They'd bury me
You'll see no strings on me

Hi Ho I'm Barry O.
I'm a puppet don't you see?
I want the world to know
Naught should ever worry thee
You'll see no strings
To make you frown
To tip my hand, with-hold my crown
I have wings
And you will see
Those angel wings on me

Dutch Puppet:
I see no strings
To worry me
We love you by the Zuider Zee
Ya Ya Ya
The Germans too
We're in the tank for you.

French Puppet:
I see no strings
Qui parle pour vous?
Les Français voient votre jeu
Je vois des cordes
Juste entre nous
Qui d'autre parle pour vous ?

Terrorist Puppet:
We in Al Qaeda know
How to make war ebb and flow
We'd like the world to know
Barry should win place and show!
(Chorus)

If I Only Had A Brain
(Wizard of Oz) EH Harburg and music by Harold Arlen

His Web is like a spider
He thinks he'll catch Al Qaeda
But watch, he's cellophane
All the while, my head I'm scratchin'
While his plans he's busy hatchin'
If he only had a brain!

He'll unravel every progress
Just like the US Congress
We soon will be in pain.
With the thoughts that he's thinkin'
He's the opposite of Lincoln
If he only had a brain!

Oh he will tell you how
The oceans are his chore
He will think of things that always stunk before
And then he'll stink! Just like Al Gore!

He seems to run on hopin'
Is that from all that dopin'?
Or is he just insane?
I could dance and be merry
If he'd just lose like John Kerry
And he'd just go down the drain!

When a man's an empty suit-er
He needs a better tutor
And yet he plays the part
He's great with written speeches
But off the cuff he reaches
If he only had the smarts!

Racial views are monumental
He seems so tempermental

Regarding kids and wife
He fosters his delusions
And he often breeds confusion
If he'd only get a life!

Picture he....a balcony
Upon a portico
Wherefore art thou, you Dumbo?
He seeks retreat
That reeks!
Just to register more voters
Honesty demoted
And then there is his wife

I will stay a bitter clinger
'Cause my rifle's a hum-dinger
And I'll guard it with my life....A Chance

Yeah, it's sad he is a sissy
His fits can be a hissy
Boy, he has arrogance!
But while terrorists are hidin'

On a rail they should be ridin'
But B.O. is just a dope!
I'm afraid there's no denyin'
He is handy when he's lyin'

Man, I think this guy's a joke!
He's a case for Jerry Springer
I'm a lone Bitter Clinger
Some would say a Vast Right Winger

And this joker won't receive this voter's vote!
'Cause I'm sure I have a brain
Some Smarts
A Life
Real HOPE

Obamalot
To the tune of "Camelot." Original by Lerner and Lowe

It's True! It's True! This Clown has made it clear
The Candidate is perfect, all must cheer!

Obama made a voter swoon, and Oh Dear!
Chris Matthews has a tingling on the spot!
Is there a regal aspect to the show here?
Obamalot?

To criticize Michelle is quite verboten
His minister's agenda he's forgot
He brings up race because he is a token

Obamalot!
Bombs a lot! Bombs a lot!
I know he sounds a bit bizarre
But Obamalot! Bombs a lot!
That's true, though he's a star.

So listen while he gives another rundown
He's great, he walks on water don't you hear?

In short there's simply not
A candidate so hot
For MSM to fawn upon than dear
Obamalot!

Obamalot!
Bombs a lot!
It surely gives a voter pause,

'Cause Obamalot! Bombs a lot!
He Hems and then he Haws!

I know he makes my stomach on the ill-side
By prime time all his campaign ads appear

In short there's simply not
A candidate so hot
For M.S.M. to fawn upon than dear
Obamalot!

It Only Takes A Moment!

Obama kept saying things like "Let this be the moment that the world healed and the oceans recede" etc. It was almost as popular as his 'yes we can' and 'hope and change' mantra. This Moment! Take a moment and contemplate what has happened now this man is elevated to POTUS of the most powerful nation on earth.
"It Only Takes a Moment" from Hello Dolly

[*Obama:*]
It only takes a moment
For your eyes to glaze and then
Your heart knows in that moment
That you'll never have to think again

I promise, for the moment
That my arms will be so strong
I can carry all the nations
And be loved my whole life long.....

[*Voters:*]
He only claims this moment
In this time, and place, but then...
Our heart knows that Obama
Surely never our world comprehends

He tells us, it's our moment
To be bold and free and strong!
So I urge you, to act boldly
And reject him, he's all Wrong!!!!

The Days of Whine and Moses
Well, he's either the Messiah or Moses. Here's the latest based on The Days of Wine and Roses (Thanks Lumberjack!)
Original song: Days of Wine and Roses, H. Mancini, J. Mercer

The Days of Whine and Moses
Have some Fun Today
He'll soon Run Away!
From his yellow plans toward a metaphor
Change is a dinosaur
We've all been there before!

This Phony Knight discloses
Nothing he's achieved
Seeks A.Q. to please!
With that golden smile, that introduced us to
The Days of Whine and Moses, poor you!

Swingin' on a Star!
From the song by Burke/Van Heusen: 'Swingin' on a Star'

Would you like to swing to the Left
Barry O. has plans for more theft
And his voters seem so obsessed
Or would you rather vote for John?

Old John's just like Barry but without funny ears
That fool seems to echo what he hears
When he thinks economy - his brain is weak
He's just a maverick - with a liberal streak
And by the way, while you think that John's a fool
Don't think his heart is miniscule!

Would you like to swing to the Right
Only John will continue the fight
But more amnesty is a blight
Or would you rather vote for Dems?

Those Dems are pathetic, they just spend all our dough
I wish they would get a clue, you know?
They've got no manners, and they blame 'Big Oil'
But drilling here will Opec profits spoil!
But if you don't think the blame is all on them
You might decide to vote for Dems

Would you like to swing to the Right
Barry O. will be No Delight
And some coat-tails might help a mite
Or would you rather just give up?

If we just surrender what will happen to us?
Gas climbing, I guess I'll take the bus!
If we give up now, and listen to those Dems
Those Carter years - We'll get to try again!
But if you think to surrender will be good
The facts you have misunderstood!

Surrender-monkeys aren't in the zoo
In our Congress there's quite a few
So you see, it's all up to you
We could be better than we are
No more Incumbents, that's a start!
We could be swingin' But we aren't!

I'm An Enemy of the State, I Am
Herman's Hermits hit "I'm Henry the Eighth, I Am"

I'm 'n Enemy of the State, I am
Enemy of the state, I am, I am
I got Harry and Pelosi to score
They'll do anything I want and more
And every one is an enemy
I wouldn't trust my cabinet or Rahm
I'm your POTUS now, and an enemy
Enemy of the state, I am, I am
Enemy of the state, I am.

I'm 'n Enemy of the State, I am
Enemy of the State, I am I am
Don't you wonder why I've opened the door
To Islamists and Hamas galore?
'Cause every one is our enemy
They don't believe in Freedom or our Land
I'm your POTUS now, and your enemy
Enemy of the state I am I am
Enemy of the state I am.
Yes I am.

Chapter Six:
Patriots, Townhallers, & Fun Stuff

They're Snide!

This was the first parody that I wrote for Townhall. It was written to deal with the many, so-called, trolls that show up on the comment section of the articles. Since Townhall is a primarily conservative site, those with more liberal views are a voice of discord to the discussions. Some are there just to irritate and highjack the thread. I learned the value of scrolling by those posts.

To all those who are frustrated by personal chats, dueling insults, getting off track from the topic and the like, I wrote the following. To the RAWHIDE theme song, original by Dimitri Tiomkin.

Scrollin', scrollin', scrollin'
Oh those libs are trollin'
Keep that mouse-wheel rollin'
They're snide!

Don't try to understand 'em
Just post, ignore and brand 'em
Soon they'll be screaming far and wide!

We recognize they're brainless
They lack logic, sense, they're aimless
But we see them as they are
'Cause they're snide

Head 'em off, let 'em shout
Keep your head, they'll just pout
We'll prevail, don't ya see they're snide?

Make your point, keep it nice
Tell 'em off, say it twice!
Head 'em off,
Drive 'em wild!
They're snide [whip crack]
They're snide! [Yee Haw!]

**alternate verse

Our finer points they're missin'
Just barking dogs and hissin'
We recognize their style
'cause they're snide.

I Get Around

From the Beach Boys, "I Get Around." Another parody to address a troll, Robert. His fantastical posts are the source of much amusement and annoyance as he seems to show up everywhere and he claims to have done everything!

I'm gettin' bugged posting up and down the same old line
I gotta finda new place where you'll think I'm just fine

My buddies and me are getting real well known
Yeah, the good guys know us and they leave us alone
I get around
No reality found
Get around round, round, I get around
I'm a real cool head
I dominate the thread
Get around round round I get around
Round
Get around round round ooooo
Wah wa OOO
Wah wa ooo oooo

I fly my helo-copter or my jet every week
Nobody else can claim to be as smart or as meek

None of the Townhalls listen cause they know I'm not right
To make such sweeping statements and to pick every fight

[*Chorus*]
Rob, Rob, say it twice
Listen to me
I've held every job on air land and sea!
Yeah
Get around round round I get around
Get around round round I get around
Wah wa ooo
Get around round round I get around

Oooo ooo ooo
Get around round round I get around
Ahh ooo ooo
Get around round round I get around
Ahh ooo ooo
Get around round round I get around
Ahh ooo ooo

Tell the Libs Off, You're the GunnyG

More on the blogosphere! GunnyG consistently writes one of the top three blogs on Townhall. Vic was my inspiration, he is a fellow writer of parodies!

From Billy Joel's "Piano Man."

It's nine o'clock on a Saturday
The regular crowd shuffles in
There's that old soldier here name of GunnyG
Tellin' Robert to go sit and spin

He says Rob, can't you refresh my memory?
I'm not really sure what you know
But you change it so often, it bears to repeat
I've forgotten more 'n you'll ever know.

La la la, de de da
La la de de da da da

(*Chorus*)

Tell the libs off, you're the GunnyG
Tell the libs off tonight
Well, we're all in the mood for your company
And you've got us feelin' all right.

Now others will chime in with things to say
Some more than others, ya know?
Some are quick with a joke or just insults to stoke
But there's no place that we'd rather be

One says, Hal, I believe you are killing me
As the smiles run away from our face
I'm sure that you could be a liberal
Why don't you get out of this place

Oh la la la, de de da

La la, de de da da da

Now lily's our resident expert
She hands out advice for free
And she shakes hands with HalD, and others like Robert
But rarely engages with me

Oh la la la, de de da
La la, de de da da da

(*Chorus*)

It's a pretty good crowd for a Saturday
And Vic will soon give us a smile
'cause we know he's great with a parody
We'll forget about life for a while.
And the threads, they devolve into bickering
And the insults they fly left and right
But we know that it's fun, even if hit and run
We say Wow! What a forum tonight!

(*Chorus*)

Do You Know What's In Store
The stem for this one is "Lookin' out My Back Door" by Creedence Clearwater Revival

Just logged on to have a chat,
Came to Townhall, lookit that!
Need to address all the libs on the thread
Confrontation sets in,
Pretty soon I'm singin'

Doo Doo Doo do you know what's in store?

There's old Robert in his helo,
And HalD is his fellow
Look at all the crazy liberals spouting all their crud
Phylo Out and lilly,
Soothsayer's a dilly

Doo Doo Doo do you know what's in store?

Conservatives and 'elephants' are taking on the Klan
Won't you add a line to our chattin' room?
(Doo Doo Doo)
Try to say with reason,
On libs its open season

Doo Doo Doo do you know what's in store?

Democrats and Liberals
Are always on the line
Won't you scroll on by,
Or just waste your time?
(Doo Doo Doo)
Insults and conflation,
Monstrous aggravation

Doo Doo Doo do you know what's in store?

Coulter brings out all the trolls,
They back their thoughts quoting polls!
Look at all those silly people bashing on Repubs!
Come again tomorrow,
Today I'll feel no sorrow.

Doo Doo Doo do you know what's in store?

How Do You Help a Liberal?

Stem: " How do You Solve a Problem like Maria" from Sound of Music, by Rodgers and Hammerstein.

A new liberal showed up soon after I began posting parodies. I wrote on my blog: "The following is the promised parody for Sophia/Devout Agnostic. This is in no way meant in a mean or nasty way as I think she presents a lucid point now and again. She is one of the few liberals on these threads that I will engage in conversation. As long as we can keep the discussion polite and respectful (no name-calling and vicious attacks) I think we all benefit from having an open mind. Challenging our beliefs is not a bad thing. With that in mind: To you, Sophia.

We begin with a chant backed up with the lead- in music to the song. You may imagine individuals from TH filling in for the Nuns, if you wish.

(Chant)
She thinks that Albert Gore
Is a lot more than a bore
She's not afraid to state her mind and scrap
She thinks that Mr. Bush
Is a simpleton, a tush
And swallows whole some other liberal pap
We've even heard her be a little nasty!
Even though it is absurd,
She hates Bush's every word.
And believes some things where reasoning is thin

Like: The Iraq war is for oil
And the earth is gonna spoil
She can dish it, and can take it on the chin
But....
I'd like to say a word in her behalf
Sophia makes me laugh!

(Cue music)

How do you help a liberal like Sophia?
How do you help her see that she is wrong?
How do you help a liberal like Sophia
A sarcastic girl that has BDS: In song?
Many the things you know
You'd like to tell her
Many the things she ought to understand
But how do you make her think
Her armor has got a chink
How do you help her leave Fantasyland?

Oh how do you help a liberal like Sophia?
Why won't she just accept a helping hand?
How do you help a liberal like Sophia?
What do you say to help a liberal out?
Sometimes she posts as Sophie, her idea
Other times she has first name Devout.

Many a time she steps on someone's toes-y
Other times she's quite content to pout
But why would she give a slight
Because we think might is right?
She fails to see what we in no way doubt.

Oh, how do you help a liberal like Sophia?
Why won't she just accept our helping hand?

Columnists are Famous

Burt Prelutsky is a popular columnist, and would make a regular appearance in the comment section to debate us as well. One day he posted he wouldn't be dropping by to post comments anymore. Many of us were sad as we enjoyed his interest in our commentary and his biting wit. He has since rethought his position, and will drop by from time to time.

I used the theme song from MASH because Burt used to write scripts for the show.

("Suicide is Painless" by Johnny Mandel and Mike Altman)

We came to Townhall and got hurt
Because of something said by Burt
He said he wouldn't stop and talk
The news 'caused all of us to balk!

'Cause columnists are famous
They very rarely claim us
And we sure do appreciate their time!

Now those of us who understood
Wrote to him to just like we should
We really tried to curb our style
We actually went the extra mile!

'Cause columnists are famous
And very rarely claim us
And we sure do appreciate their time!

So Burt come back we miss your smile
We miss your posts we miss your style
We surely welcome you to stay
Don't take your quips and clips away!

'Cause columnists are famous
And very rarely claim us
We surely do appreciate your time!

Come back sometime!
Please drop in and opine!

Scroll on By
More on trolls: Dionne Warwick's hit "Walk on By" by Burt Bacharach

If you see them posting on the thread
And they start to say
The GOP's dead
Scroll on by, scroll on by

Make believe
That's what they choose to post
Why won't they leave?
Don't feed them 'cause each time you see them
They'll your patience try
Just scroll on by (don't stop)
Just scroll on by (don't stop)
Just scroll on by

They just can't get over a Bush Two
And still they remain,
Broken and Blue
Scroll on by, scroll on by

Foolish pride
That's all that they have left
Why don't they hide?
They won't even listen to reason
So I'll say goodbye
and Scroll on by
and scroll on by
(don't stop)

My wheel rolls, my wheel rolls
Foolish trolls
They don't believe a word
So my wheel scrolls
By anger and words without logic
Just tell them goodbye
Scroll on by (don't stop)
and scroll on by (don't stop)
and scroll on by (don't stop)

Rob Rob Rob

On April 19, 2008, I wrote the following:

I've been getting bugged lately by the sheer volume of posts by, or devoted to, Robert. I guess I support his right to post his drivel as many times and as often as he wishes, but there seems to be a growing cult-like anti-Robert group that just piles on and on and on with Robert as the subject. I'd prefer to discuss the columns and so my scroll wheel is getting worn out. So here is my song to you Townhallers. Thanks to the Beach Boys...I think you'll recognize the (medley) of tunes.

Rob Rob Rob Rob Rob's your man
Rob Rob Rob Rob Rob's your man
Rob Rob Rob Rob Rob's your man

I'm getting bugged scrollin' up and down the same old threads
You've gotta find a new way! Address the column instead!
(Guitar)
Rob and his buddy Hal D are gettin' real well known
All the smart guys know them and they leave them alone
They get around
Only insanity found
They echo what they said
They clutter up the thread

Rob Rob Rob Rob Rob's your man
Rob Rob Rob Rob Rob's your man
Rob Rob Rob Rob Rob's your man

I always take the time to read Townhall every week
But when I get to the threads it's not old Robert I seek
(Guitar)
All the Townhall bloggers seem to egg on the fight
And with the insults flyin' they just seem to delight
In piling on
Til the column is gone

It doesn't make him leave
He has more up his sleeve

Rob Rob Rob Rob Rob's your man
Rob Rob Rob Rob Rob's your man
Rob Rob Rob Rob Rob's your man

OOOOOOO EEEE I just wish you could see.....eeeee
That he....eee Just likes celebrity ....eeee
OOOOO EEEEEE (*fade*)

Nobody Likes a Liberal Like Sophia

This is a re-mix following a multitude of run-ins with the moderators and others on Townhall. Sophia's handle has morphed many times, the most recent being "Everybody Loves Sophie." I'm sure that she sees the irony of this moniker, as she has lost favor with most of us who originally enjoyed the repartee..

To the tune of "How Do you Solve a Problem Like Maria" from Sound of Music. (This supercedes the original parody to Sophia)

[Chant]
She thinks that Barry O
Hopes for her support, and so
She comes to Townhall to rabble rouse and scrap

She also thinks that Bush
Is a simpleton, a tush
And swallows whole that other liberal crap

But lately she's been getting awfully nasty!

Even though it is absurd
She hates Bush's every word
And believes some things where reasoning is dim

Obama-Nation gets her toil
And from 'fundies' she recoils
She can dish it, but our patience has grown thin
Yikes!....
I once would say a word in her behalf
She used to make me laugh!

(cue music)
Nobody likes a liberal like Sophia
Nobody wants to listen to her swill
Nobody likes a liberal like Sophia
A provocateur, an Obama hack, a Shill

Many a man has tried to reason with her
Many a post is flagged because it's vile
But why should we then engage
She just wants us to enrage
Why did she ever tend to make me smile?

Oh Nobody likes a liberal like Sophia
She's one among the liberal rank and file.

Nobody likes a liberal like Sophia
Nobody likes a voice that is so shrill
Nobody likes a liberal like Sophia
That hatred for Bush and Coulter,
A poison pill
Many the mountain she makes out of molehills
Highjacking threads just gives our Sophie thrills

But why would we seek to play?
Or listen to what she says?
She's 'Stuck on Stupid' Yes, that fits the bill

Oh nobody likes a liberal like Sophia
If we ignore her, go away she will.

Tony Snow

There are some people who just cannot hide their light under a bushel. Tony Snow was one of those men. I never met him, but I felt I knew who he was and what he was about. I greatly admired him, and his loss is deeply felt. My heart goes out to his family and friends. Would that we all could leave this world with the sense that we made a difference. Here was a true 'uniter,' for even those who disagreed with his philosophy could not find it in their hearts to hate this man. What a legacy!

Here's my tribute to Tony Snow.
Based on the Christmas Carol "Let It Snow"
by Sammy Cahn and Jule Styne.

All together he was insightful
And his smile was so delightful
And we all admired him so.
Tony Snow, Tony Snow, Tony Snow

It doesn't seem fair to lose him
'Cause Bush was right to choose him.
But God has him now, we know.
Tony Snow, Tony Snow, Tony Snow

When he finally shared his plight
How we prayed he could weather the storm!
And we hate that he lost the fight
All of us share as we mourn

The shock is slowly dying,
And we all are still good-bye-ing
His integrity surely showed
Tony Snow, Tony Snow,
So-Long, Snow.

Love a Pun

Just for fun I wrote a response to a fellow poster, Savage99, who was giving me a hard time about using puns. (I know it is the 'lowest form of humor' but I like them!)

From the original "Still the One" by John Joseph Hall and Johanna D. Hall.

I've been a poster since way back when
Sometimes my humor is *by the pen*
But I want you to know, since I love to joke
Don't be surprised if your eye I sometimes *poke*!

(Chorus)

I love a pun – And I know it's *low*
But the pun – *lifts* my heart so
I'm always having fun, and I love a pun!

I love to give *'stitches'* to all of you
But I guess it *requires a point* of view
When insults came, I just wanted to go
(wanted to go)
Far from old Townhall,
But I longed for humor, *'sew'*...

(Chorus)

Cos it's just a pun – that makes me laugh
Just a pun – Better far by half
It's just having fun, and I love a pun
Cos it's just a pun – a play with words
Just a pun – a melody absurd
I'm just having fun, and I love a pun!

Changing my humor to suit you--
It won't be the same-
To my own self I'm true

I Love a Pun –It's a joke with *class*
Love a Pun – It's *first* to make me laugh
I'm still having fun, and I love a pun

It is just a pun –That keeps you *sharp*
Just a pun –that makes a *dullard* smart
I'm still having fun, cos I love a pun

I just love a pun, yeah love a pun
I'm still having Pun and I love the Fun!

He's Just Absurd!
The next three poems, were written to respond to challenges from my friend, Curtal Friar.
This one is from Grease:" Grease is the Word" by Frankie Valli

Who'll solve your problems if you 'see the light?'
Who's gonna run, you think, if we don't keep it right?
Ain't there some danger he can go too far?
He must be leaving now, so we can be who we are
He's Just Absurd!

He wants our government to centralize
Why don't he understand that we see his disguise?
He keeps on lying, but we must be real
We need to question why he's gotten so much appeal!
He's just absurd!
(He's just absurd, just absurd, that's the word)
He will prove he's left-leaning
(We've got no time in this race for this notion)
We on the Right see it keenly.

We take his measure and we hit the wall
His personality belongs in basketball
If there's a chance that he can win the whole thing
We'll just start grieving now; you folks will buy anything!
He's just absurd!
(He's just absurd, just absurd, that's the word)
He will prove he's left-leaning
(We've got no time in this race for this notion)
We on the Right see it keenly.

All of his lies are Illusion
Wrapped up in Trouble
Race and Confusion
How did we get here?

How do we ensure we save the day?
Our nationality belongs to 'all,' we say
We don't want anyone to change the tune
Oh say, our anthem's fine, and we don't need a buffoon
He's just absurd!
(He's just absurd, just absurd, that's the word)
He will prove he's left-leaning
(We've got no time in this race for this notion)
We on the Right see it keenly.

He's just absurd!
(He's just absurd, just absurd, that's the word)
He will prove he's left-leaning
(We've got no time in this race for this notion)
We on the Right see it keenly.
He's just absurd
Is absurd, Is absurd, Is absurd.....*(repeat & fade)*

America Vs Al Qaeda
The Royal Guardsmen "Snoopy V the Red Baron"

After the turn of the century
From the clear blue skies in New York City
Came a roar and a thunder men there'd never heard
And we screamed as the towers turned into potsherds

Up in the sky, in flight Ninety-Three
More terrorists rode into infamy
Four men tried and forty-four died
In that plane in the Pennsylvania countryside

Ten, twenty, thirty, forty, fifty or more
Those Bloody Al Qaedas were hoping to score
Many men died at the end of that spree
Of the Bloody Al Qaedas of infamy

In the thick of the smoke, a hero stood tall
His name was George Bush and he rallied us all
We knew that this guy didn't seek revenge
But to guarantee all it wouldn't happen again.

Ten, twenty, thirty, forty, fifty or more
Those Bloody Al Qaedas were hoping to score
Many folks died at the end of that spree
Of the Bloody Al Qaedas of Infamy

Now, Dubya took the war to the Taliban
Then he went to the Congress for a new battle plan
Hussein was bad and so we called his bluff
And a coalition formed to say enough was enough.

That Bloody Al Qaeda woke a sleeping bear
And the Bush doctrine said we'd rather fight them there
We kicked some butt; our cause is right
And some bad guys tasted some American might!

Ten, Twenty, Thirty, Forty, Fifty or more
The Bloody Al Qaedas were hoping to score
Many Men died tryin' to end that spree
Of the Bloody Al Qaeda of Infamy

Midnight in Montana
*This isn't a parody, and it isn't even political,
but this is my book so I put it in!
It is the result of a challenge from my friend Curtal Friar
to write a Sestina using six words and a title that he
gave me. A new idea for poetry, at least new to me!
A Sestina has a certain form. (Look it up! I did!)*

*Here is my Sestina, based on CF's suggested title:
Midnight in Montana, with six words: Dark, Light,
Sheepdog, Dandelion, Moon and Coyote.*

Upon a midnight in Montana dark
I saw the peaks bereft of light
Surprised, I came upon a sheepdog
His ruffled fur as golden as a dandelion;
Bristly and washed to grey by the moon
And in the air the howl of a coyote.

The dog lifted his head to hear the coyote.
His eyes gleamed like a golden moon
I fancied he must be a dandy lion!
Seeing not the faithful sheepdog
Who crouched upon a Montana dark
At midnight, hidden from the light.

A midnight moon bestowed its light
Magical, illumines rocks bright and shadows dark
Planting shadows of tree and dandelion
Shaggy as he: the sheepdog,
Undisturbed by a yip from a coyote
As he howls and bays at the moon.

All silent and still the silver moon
Glowing on high for the coyote
A voice as it echoes across the Montana dark
Whispers of intrigues and shared delight!

What hears the canine? the faithful old sheepdog?
As he rests in a meadow of dandelion?

In the daytime, a field full of golden dandelion
Undulates like a river of light
As golden and bright as a white midnight moon
And no sign in its blooms of the coyote.
He seems more at home in the midnight dark
Far removed from his cousin the sheepdog.

Midnight in Montana hides a sheepdog
A shadow, an echo, a cousin in light
And he shares much in common with the coyote.
A howl floats like seeds from a dandelion
Wafting upwards to touch the moon
Bewailing the passing of the dark.

And what value light? and what mystery moon?
Inside Montana dark lies the world of the coyote.
He's the real Dandy Lion going after the sheep! Dawg!

Someday When We See Rainbows

I read an article about another Obama supporter from Illinois, Reverend Meeks, who was called on the carpet for his inflammatory remarks of equating politicians with slave-masters over minorities. He used the term 'house-niggers.' He later excused the use of the offensive term by saying it was 'acceptable' as a term of 'endearment' within the black community. He later signed onto the Rainbow/PUSH decision to bury the 'N' word.

Originally, according to the Bible, the Rainbow was God's sign that he would never cover the earth with flood-waters again. This symbol has been usurped by both race-baiters like Jesse Jackson (Rainbow/PUSH) and the gay community as their flag and symbol of 'diversity.'

From the Wizard of Oz, "Somewhere Over the Rainbow" original music by Harold Arlen and lyrics by E. Y. Harburg.

Nowadays when we see rainbows
Way up high
Though it once was God's symbol
Others now mis-apply.

Someday when we see rainbows
We'll be blue
And those dreams that King dared to dream
Never will come true

If we elect Obama czar
We'll wake up with our best days far
Behind us
When we go into culture shock
We'll recognize this poppycock
Was just some stardust

Someday when we see rainbows
Adonai
Will again claim His symbol
His Name be Glorified!

If we elect Obama czar
We'll wake up with our best days far
Behind us
When we go into culture shock
We'll recognize this poppycock
Was just some stardust

Someday when we see rainbows
Adonai
Will again claim His symbol
His Name be Glorified!

If we will turn to Adonai
Embrace His rainbow
He will bring us nigh!

He Is Your Friend

My mom was the most extraordinary person in my life. Her favorite hymn was "What a Friend We Have in Jesus." With thanks to God, I have re-written James Taylor's wonderful song lyrics to reflect that sentiment. From James Taylor "You've Got a Friend"

When you're down and troubled,
And you need a helping hand
And nothing, no nothing is going right
Close your eyes and say a prayer
He always will be there
To lighten up even your darkest night

You just call out His name
And you know, whenever you do
He will listen, oh yeah, brother
He will see you through
Winter, spring, summer or fall,
All you have to do is call
And He'll be there, yeah, yeah, yeah.
He is your friend.

If the world around you
Seems all dark and full of doubts
And you think that nobody sees or knows
Bow your head in silence
And call His name out low
He is there, just knocking upon your door

You just call out His name
And you know He'll listen and care
All your burdens He gladly will share
In your doubt, pain or despair
He will listen to your prayer
And He'll be there, yeah, yeah, yeah.
Now til the end.

Hey ain't it good to know
That you've got a friend
When people can be so cold
He won't hurt you nor e'er desert you
He'll save your soul if you let Him
Oh yeah, Why don't you let Him?

You just call out His name
And you know He'll listen and care
All your burdens He gladly will share
In your doubt, pain or despair
He will listen to your prayer
And He'll be there, yes He will.
Now til the end.

You've got a friend.

Ain't it good to know He is your friend.
Ain't it good to know He is your friend.
He is your friend.

We Built This Country
*From Starship, "We Built This City" Original
by Bernie Taupin & Martin Page.
I wrote this parody in December 2007 before
the nominations were finalized.*

We built this country!
We built this country on Freedom's soil
We built this country on Freedom's soil

Say you don't worry, Our Constitution's strong
Why don't you want to say, who's right and who's wrong?
Knee deep in the campaign, who will get the nod?
Too many candidates and all of them are flawed.

Obama spars with Clinton, Rush is on the
radio, don't you remember?
We built this country, we built this country on freedom's soil!
We built this country, we built this country on freedom's soil!
Built this country, built this country on freedom's soil!

Someone's always playing their campaigning games
Who cares they're always slinging Mud on others' names
We just want our country to go on being free
Won't you be responsible, Won't you speak for me?

Mitt Romney spars with Rudy, Rush is on
the radio, don't you remember?
We built this country, we built this country on freedom's soil!
We built this country, we built this country on freedom's soil!
Built this country, built this country on freedom's soil!

It's just another campaign
On a four year plan
Clinton has got a choke hold
So says the anchorman

How can we stop her? Do we have a plan?
Don't say you won't go vote! We must find our man!
Don't tell me you're climbing aboard the ship of fools
We must save America our tradition rules

*[I'm looking out over the United States. Need a victory
on election day! No more RINO or Demo Republic!]*

Don't you remember ('member, 'member)

*[What's your favorite candidate, in your favorite country? The country
where we're free, the country that rocks! The country of Liberty!]*

Obama spars with Clinton, Rush is on the
radio, Don't you remember?
We built this country, we built this country on freedom's soil!
We built this country, we built this country on freedom's soil!
Built this country, built this country on freedom's soil!
Built this country, built this country on freedom's soil!
Built this country, built this country on freedom's soil!

(We Built, we built this country) Built this
country (we built, we built this country)
(*repeat and fade*)

Sweet USA
Based on Neil Diamond's "Sweet Caroline"

When we began
Thanks to our Patriot Fathers!
Foundations make our country strong

Was an idea
That grew to be a nation
Who'd a believed we'd come along?
Hands, working hands
Reachin out
Building lives!
Living free!

Sweet USA!
All our days just seem so good
We've been inclined
To believe they always would

But now I
Look at our state
And it don't seem as solid
We wonder if it will remain.
We don't need change
Changin' will hurt our nation
Why choose to change to something strange?

Seek, Liberty
We must fight
For the Right
To be Free!

Sweet USA
All our days just seem so good
We've been inclined
To believe they always would.

Oh, no, no
Sweet USA
Every day here is so good
Don't be so blind
To believe it always would

Sweet USA (repeat and fade)

Our Great Liberty
This soaring song cries out for a little Patriotic feeling! I hope you enjoy it! "Circle of Life" From the Lion King, music and lyrics by Elton John and Tim Rice

[Chant]
Come on our life is just so sweet here
Oh yes, the USA's a leader
(repeat)

[begin music]

From the day we arrived in this nation
Where from many, we became One
We've loved liberty and equality
To defend our home has got to be done!

There's too much at stake to surrender
For defense, we must remain strong
Hold your banners high
Say "Live Free or Die"
Raise your voice in pledge and in song!

We enjoy living free
And it lifts us all
From despair into hope
With faith and love
Til a beacon we'll be
The whole world yearning
For our Freedom!
Our Great Liberty!

We enjoy living Free!
And it lifts us all
From Despair into Hope
With Faith and Love!
Til a beacon we'll be
The whole world yearning
For our Freedom!
Our Great Liberty!

Printed in the United States
146479LV00003B/47/P